NEVER SAY DIE
THE REMARKABLE RISE OF EXETER CITY

Nick Spencer

Published by Nick Spencer
First published November 2009
© Nick Spencer

ISBN 978–0–9564193–0–9

A catalogue record for this book is available from the British Library.

A number of photographs appear throughout this book.
Front cover: Keith Stone and Andrew Payne.
Thanks to Phil Mingo/Pinnacle Photography Ltd (www.ppauk.com), Exeter City club photographer prior to 2006 (including Michael Jackson, Brazil and Manchester United pictures).
Special thanks to Keith Stone, Exeter City's club photographer since 2006 (www.cheggerspics.co.uk)
John Barnes/Paul Tisdale picture courtesy of *Southern Daily Echo*.
Wembley posters courtesy of Ashley House Printing Co., Exeter.

Book design by Kevin Bovey.

Typeset, printed and bound by Kingfisher Print & Design Ltd, Wills Road, Totnes Industrial Estate, Totnes, Devon TQ9 5XN.

Front cover: Conference play-off final, Wembley 2007;
Exeter manager Paul Tisdale celebrates promotion, 2009.
Back cover: Rob Edwards, Wembley 2008.

CONTENTS

I was born in Bradford, spent my early childhood as an army brat in Cyprus, Bahrain and Uganda, my teenage years in East Yorkshire, and most of my early working life in London . . . so why the hell do I support Exeter City? Well, like most of the good things in life – it was an accident.

I've supported a few teams in my life: Bradford Park Avenue as a kid in the sixties, Hull City as a teenager in the seventies, the eighties I spent chasing wine, women and song, and in the nineties I was living 200 yards from Stamford Bridge so I went along and watched Chelsea. I like football as a game.

I started watching City in the same way. Having moved to the West Country I needed a football fix and a mate suggested we go and watch City's fight to stay in the league at the end of the 2002/03 season. We couldn't get in, but having made the effort to get there we watched the game perched on a shopping trolley in one of the gardens behind the away end.

There were a lot of people watching alongside us and the atmosphere was superb. Someone had a radio on so we could listen to the Swansea game at the same time. I went along for the laugh, for the spectacle, to see the excitement of success or failure, and though it was ultimately a miserable result for City, I had a really good day out.

Then came the Manchester United games and the joy of watching Ronaldo taking corners against the backdrop of an advert for Ivor Dewdney pasties . . . and I got slowly hooked. Not by the quality of the football, which really wasn't very good at first, but by the sight of people actually trying. I fell in love with the endeavour, with the passion people showed, with people scrapping to survive as a club.

I got myself a season ticket, and went to the odd away game near London. But the real turning point was joining the Supporters' Trust. I don't *do* anything as such, I just pay my subs, but there is something completely different about owning a bit of the club you support. All right, they haven't asked me to select the team yet, nor have they played my aggressive 'reverse Christmas tree'

formation, but it's a totally different atmosphere. It brings with it a sense of community and shared purpose that I haven't experienced anywhere else. When something as simple as clearing your own cups and rubbish away after the game gives you the feeling that you're genuinely helping to save the club, what's not to like?

And it's been an exhilarating few years, both on and off the pitch – as this book shows! What a journey. What excitement. When Nick asked me to write this foreword I asked him to send me the first chapter so that I could get a flavour of what he was writing, but he sent me the full manuscript, and I simply couldn't put it down. It's a brilliant story, with the narrative arc of a Hollywood movie. All it needs to make it complete, perhaps, is for City to win the Premiership . . . Come on! You've got to dream!

Adrian Edmondson

It's the last day of the 2008/09 season, and in a League Two match against Rotherham United in the incongruous setting of Sheffield's Don Valley Athletics Stadium, Exeter City have a corner.

There are 19 minutes left and 2,454 Exeter fans are gathered behind the goal Exeter have been attacking with increasing conviction, desperately willing them on in their quest for the goal that would assure their promotion to League One.

Out on the Exeter left, midfielder Ryan Harley plays a short corner to Rob Edwards. Every one of those 2,454 fans urges the ageless Edwards to sling the ball into the Rotherham penalty area, but he buys himself a little more time and plays the ball back to Harley, who returns the favour.

Every vanishing second heightens the tension among the supporters. Then, after what seems an eternity, Edwards looks up and arrows a perfect cross beyond the far post. Substitute Richard Logan has timed his run from the right wing to perfection, easily outjumps the Rotherham full-back and heads the ball neatly past goalkeeper Andy Warrington.

Looking back, it all seems so straightforward. Exeter travelled to Sheffield, temporary home of Rotherham United, requiring a win from their final game of the season to secure a second successive promotion. A simple equation. But this is Exeter City we are talking about. Six years earlier, give or take a day, they had slipped out of the Football League, after 83 years' unbroken membership, amid a welter of recrimination, farce and far, far worse.

In 2009 it fell to Richard Logan to write his name in Exeter's history book, though it could have been one of any number of heroes. Sent on by the Exeter manager, Paul Tisdale, with the words 'go and score the winning goal' ringing in his ears, Logan followed his instructions to the glorious letter.

This is the story of one of the most remarkable turnarounds of a club in the modern game. There is no such thing as six short years in the ultra competitive world of professional football, and the amount of effort expended to save a club whose death rattle was clearly audible during the summer of 2003 has been an inspiration. There is a hint in this tale of Asterix the Gaul, in which a small but indomitable band take on the might of the Roman Empire and triumph in spite of insurmountable

odds. All that is missing is the magic potion. Did I mention that City missed a penalty against Rotherham that would have made the final 10 minutes a joyous party rather than an agonising wait? But that's Exeter for you, a club not given to choosing the easy path.

This book is dedicated to all the people who decided that Exeter City FC was just too important to be allowed to wither away. To the managers and players, whose deeds on the pitch exceeded all expectations, probably even their own; to the people who worked tirelessly behind the scenes, often for no money; and to the supporters who put their hands in their pockets, often to the tune of hundreds of pounds each, to save the club, joined the Supporters' Trust and followed the team all over the country knowing that they owned a little part of it.

In short, this book is for everyone who has played his or her part in the revitalisation of Exeter City, the club that refused to die.

Nick Spencer
September 2009

Nick Spencer is a sports journalist for *The Daily Telegraph* and has reported on more than 1,000 club and international matches. He watched his first game at St James Park in September 1979.

Although exiled from Devon, he has done his best to ensure coverage of Exeter City in the national press. He lives in south west London.

ACKNOWLEDGEMENTS

When the idea for this book began to crystallise in my mind on 2 May 2009, possibly in a desperate attempt to distract my thoughts from what might be about to unfold at the Don Valley Stadium, I knew there was a host of brilliant stories to tell. How well they have been recorded for posterity it is for the reader to judge, but the book would not have appeared at all without the considerable help of a small army of people.

It may be chance that so many articulate players have represented Exeter City in recent seasons; but then again, maybe not. All the players I have interviewed have been unfailingly helpful and if the story it lives on the page, it is thanks to their recollections and opinions.

One of the prime reasons for attempting the book in the first place was the quality of photographs taken by the club photographer, Keith 'Cheggers' Stone, and the evidence is there for all to see. His predecessor, Phil Mingo, has been extraordinarily generous in allowing the use of his archive. Many of the stories recounted in these pages were first aired on the *Express and Echo* website and on the club's internet show, *Kellow's Bootlaces*.

Considerable thanks must go to an excellent copy-editor, Daniel Balado-Lopez, and to the staff of Kingfisher, in Totnes, who designed and printed the book. Thanks also to my mother, Felicity Cawthra, for suggesting the title, and to Jessica McCarthy, my sister, and Andrew Payne for countless pieces of good advice. Also to David Treharne and Peter Evans for their considerable efforts in trying to ensure I got the facts right.

I have heard the phrase 'labour of love' a great deal but I came to realise that, in trying to write a book and work full-time, I briefly had something in common with those supporters who put their lives on hold to save Exeter City in 2003. This may explain the fund of goodwill towards the club and pride in their achievements, as Adrian Edmondson captures so beautifully in his foreword. Having been an 'exile' for too many years, the generosity I have benefited from has been incontrovertible proof that you get a better class of person in Devon.

Numerous people have contributed in so many ways to the process of writing the book – too numerous to mention. However, particular thanks must go to Julian Tagg, Steve Perryman and Paul Tisdale for their help and support, not least for reading various drafts in search of the inevitable factual errors. Paul Tisdale gave up his valuable time, quite beyond any reasonable expectation, and displayed an attention to detail that will come as no surprise to any supporter of the club.

Finally, thank you for buying the book, and if your part in the rise and rise of Exeter City is not reflected in these pages it is only because there have been so many of you.

Nick Spencer

t is not hard to identify the worst day in the history of Exeter City Football Club. Far from looking forward to celebrating their centenary year, the club's very existence was in jeopardy after they became the first victims of the Football League's decision to relegate two clubs to the Nationwide Conference. Not even three successive wins to end the season could save them.

Nine thousand people, or at least those who managed to get inside St James Park before the police insisted the gates be closed, turned up to witness the death throes of the club's membership of the Football League. Some were casual observers, drawn by the inherent drama of a club battling for its status, but most of those with a deeper loyalty will have walked away from the ground numb with disappointment but also wondering how on earth the club had ended up in this position.

True to the recent history of the Grecians, there were chaotic scenes outside and inside St James Park. In fact, over the course of a season which began with Uri Geller and Michael Jackson (billed, improbably, as an honorary director) bringing some unaccustomed publicity to this homely West Country club, just one more point would have kept them in the Football League and spared everyone the immediate agony. But at what possible future cost it was impossible to guess.

The End of an Era

Exeter City 1 (Flack 90) **Southend 0**

Exeter: Miller; Hiley, Gaia (Kilheeney 70), Baker, Todd; Coppinger, Walker, Ampadu (Cronin 77), Pettefer; Flack, Devine.
Subs: Fraser (g), Roscoe, McConnell

Southend: Flahavan; Beard, Cort, McSweeney, Searle; Darby (Thurgood 11), Strachan, Maher, Jenkins; Rawle (Kightly 87), Bramble.
Subs: Gay (g), Henry, Salter

Referee: M. Fletcher

Attendance: 9,036

A more sombre way to end 83 years' unbroken League service it would be difficult to imagine, with a raucous knot of Southend supporters confirming Swansea's victory 10 minutes before Steve Flack's winning goal.

Exeter had diced with this most precarious game of musical chairs before. In 1995 they finished

Exeter winger James Coppinger is outnumbered against Southend.

last, but Macclesfield's lack of a ground certificate saved them. That 2002/03 season, with new men John Russell and Mike Lewis in charge, boasting some grandiose plans, and the recruitment, however fleeting, of big, albeit fading, playing names like Lee Sharpe and Don Goodman, such problems had seemed unthinkable. But two managers were dispensed with: John Cornforth too soon, and Neil McNab too late. Even after 17 points from 12 games under Gary Peters, yet another manager, City's fate rested largely in South Wales in the hands of Peter Taylor, a man whose playing career had ebbed away at St James Park under Gerry Francis 20 years earlier, and his erratic Hull team.

Play started on time at the Vetch Field, but at Exeter the kick-off was put back 15 minutes. News soon filtered through of a Swansea lead followed by a Hull equaliser.

When play finally started at St James Park, Southend made the most of the strong wind to pin Exeter back until, after six minutes, disaster appeared to have struck when an untidy challenge by City's Carl Pettefer gave Southend a penalty. Tesfaye Bramble, lesser-known brother of then Newcastle defender Titus, took it but goalkeeper Kevin Miller, not for the first time in his distinguished City career, beat away the shot. Crisis averted.

Fans show their support for Exeter after the game.

Two supporters share the pain of relegation.

Moments later came news that Hull were 2–1 ahead in South Wales. For the time being at least, Exeter were in 90th place and safe, with the doughty Miller continuing to deal with whatever Southend could throw at him.

How much the City players knew of the two goals Swansea scored while half-time was being taken at St James Park was impossible to tell, but the crowd were understandably deflated by the time they returned for the second half. Even an Exeter win would not save them now, only Hull doing something improbable. They didn't, eventually subsiding to a 4–2 defeat.

Exeter plugged away gamely and Pettefer and Flack both tested the Southend goalkeeper, Darryl Flahavan, but relegation had already been confirmed by the final whistle on Swansea's victory as the club which gave us Fred Binney, Tony Kellow and Darran Rowbotham struggled to produce a modern marksman to match. In added time they found one – Flack rounded Flahavan to score from a tight angle – but it was all to no avail.

'I am devastated,' said Peters. 'I cannot believe it. I do not know what more I could have done. There have been so many late goals and pieces of

bad luck. Without them we would have been safe weeks ago. It's going to be a long, horrible summer for the players.'

How right he was.

Eyewitness

The third of May 2003 should have been the greatest day in the lives of Neil and Julie Le Milliere as they tied the knot on the pitch at St James Park. Engaged 15 months earlier, Julie had suggested the hallowed turf to Neil, a lifelong Exeter fan, as the ideal place for a blessing, little knowing what awaited them.

> *The happiest day of our lives? Well, it could have been. We would have been happy with the thought of celebrating our wedding after another season of mid-table mediocrity. Neil was involved in the Supporters' Trust and knew of some of the niggles behind the scenes but he took his role seriously and wouldn't tell me. Just before the wedding, Neil was asked to make out his deposit as a personal cheque but he refused and made it out to the club.*
>
> *After a small Register Office ceremony, we made our way to the ground with 140 guests for what was possibly the longest day of my life. That's when I really started to get nervous about the game. I think we just knew and were quite glad to have something else to focus on.*
>
> *After a blessing on the pitch, which was filmed by Sky and a Dutch TV station, we headed for the buffet. Neil had an inkling that something might go awry, and when someone checked, people were sitting in our seats – they had been sold twice. Neil quickly got everyone out and into their seats.*
>
> *The ground was packed to the rafters but it was the quietest City game I've ever been to. We knew before the final whistle we were down. We were just numb, and then I thought, Oh God, we've got a wedding reception now. The majority of our guests were either Exeter fans or football fans in general, who understood our pain.*
>
> *It was a brilliant night, though. We had a ceilidh band and a disco and everyone got very drunk, which at least put everything off until the following morning. Everyone woke up with the same thought: it wasn't a nightmare, we really have been relegated.*
>
> *One thing that really pleased me was that we were late paying the club for the tickets and I am so glad that Russell and Lewis had gone by the time we sent off the cheque.*

Uri Geller sheds a tear at the end of the Southend game as City are relegated.

Michael Jackson arrives on the pitch at St James Park by vintage car.

Russell and Lewis

If the Southend game and relegation marked a new low point for Exeter, the most fateful day in the club's history was the one a year earlier when John Russell and Mike Lewis rode into town looking for a football club to run.

They were both 'football men', although their CVs did not look promising. Russell had been the owner and chairman of Scarborough from 1994 to 2000. When he resigned, following relegation to the Conference, the club was insolvent and owed creditors £1.25 million. Lewis had worked in the commercial departments of several clubs, including Reading, but he described his brief spell as managing director of Swansea City as 'a complete disaster'. Swansea ended up insolvent with debts of £1.7 million, and for a time Lewis believed his safety was in danger from angry fans.

In 2002, the Football League did not have a 'fit and proper person' test to check the credentials of so-called businessmen who wanted to take over struggling clubs. Had such a test been in place Russell would have been barred, because in March 1999 he had received a 15-month prison sentence, suspended for two years, after pleading guilty in Leeds Crown Court to obtaining property by deception in a £180,000 hire-purchase fraud.

Russell and Lewis had first tried Lincoln City, but were rebuffed by a newly formed supporters' trust. At Exeter, however, Ivor Doble, a local businessman

Uri Geller and Michael Jackson, complete with City scarf, on the London train.

who had helped to bankroll the club for years and had loaned it almost half a million pounds, was approaching 80 and was desperate to hand over the reins. Fatefully, he struck a deal to give Russell and Lewis control.

The pair's first months at the club were marked by a blaze of publicity, including an improbable

Michael Jackson meets a young fan.

Mike Lewis and John Russell.

How Had it Come to This?

There's a hoary old football anecdote that is so ridiculous it probably has its roots in reality. It concerns a newly appointed director of a club who asked one of the old guard what the guiding principles should be. 'Forget everything you ever learned in business,' came the reply, which probably explains a lot.

John Russell and Mike Lewis ran Exeter City for a year and left it on the brink of ruination. They may have proved hopeless at running a business but they certainly had a nose for publicity, most of it unwelcome.

Even before the wild talk of recruiting Paul Gascoigne as player-manager, Uri Geller, the walking publicity machine and celebrity spoonbender, was named 'co-chairman'; he, in turn, recruited Michael Jackson as an 'honorary director' (soon to be joined by actor Dave 'Darth Vader' Prowse) and persuaded him to headline undoubtedly the strangest performance St James Park will ever witness.

One hundred fans paid £100 each to board the Exeter Express at Paddington station with Jackson, who, partially hidden under a large umbrella for protection from the sun, eventually appeared at the ground in a vintage car for a fund-raising event for the club and local charities. A tour of the ground had been planned, but in the confusion the car's path became blocked by media and fans after about 100 yards.

Jackson spoke for several minutes about 'this great football club', his support for the children of the world and his desire to end AIDS, malaria and war. 'We must learn to live and love each other before it's too late,' he said, before urging everyone at the ground to 'hold hands with your neighbour and tell them that you love them'. As a feature of City home games it never really caught on. Unfortunately, time did not permit him to expound his views on the merits of a 4-4-2 system versus 5-3-2.

A successful day? Well, the world still has its problems and Jackson never did return to watch a game. Nor was it entirely a triumph for the club. Some months later a £9,000 bill for the train arrived, and in the corner of the pitch where the stage had been erected, a drain broke. The programme makers of Jackson's appearance instructed bailiffs. The new regime might have put Exeter on the map, but this bizarre event sowed the seeds of City's financial collapse.

move to install Paul Gascoigne as player-manager, so perhaps it was appropriate that David Blaine and Uri Geller, two of the world's most famous illusionists, were involved, as things were not as they seemed. When their case eventually came to trial, Russell would plead guilty to the charge that he 'dishonestly obtained for himself . . . membership of the board of Exeter City AFC by deception, namely by falsely representing that he had substantial funds to introduce to the club'.

Paul Majendie travelled to Exeter from London on a train with Michael Jackson to cover the American's visit to St James Park on 14 June 2002 and found himself sitting in a car next to the 'King of Pop'. It was, he says, the most surreal day he can remember in a long career as a showbusiness reporter for Reuters.

> *On that train were three of the biggest weirdos on God's earth, Jackson, Uri Geller and David Blaine – one of the most pretentious men on the planet. Girls were offering 'jollities and mirth' to get into Jackson's carriage.*

I would put that day right up there with interviewing Paul McCartney and covering Madonna's wedding, though I spent the whole day trying not to burst out laughing. I've never enjoyed a day so much.

Even before we left, Jackson impressed me when girls surrounded him on Paddington station and he was jostled: his survival training kicked in and he just dropped to the floor and 'disappeared', crawled away. A lot of celebrities are taught that because it confuses all the fans just long enough to get away.

When we arrived in Exeter I was in the second of two blacked-out limousines. He always had a camera crew with him for insurance purposes, and the cameraman had a glove on. Every so often I got him to put his gloved hand through the sliding roof of the car as we careered through the streets of Exeter and the crowds screamed, obviously thinking it was Jackson himself.

After that bizarre performance at the football ground it was rather like a Papal audience as he met a line of disabled children. For one horrible moment I thought, He's going to bless them.

As we were about to leave the ground, I rushed down the steps and jumped into the car, and when I looked up I found I was sitting next to Michael Jackson. It was the wrong car! I apologised, but he said very quietly, 'That's no problem at all,' and I scuttled out.

On the way home, Uri duly obliged and bent a spoon. I was very jealous of one of my colleagues as she kept it and he wouldn't do it twice because he said it would drain him of energy.

On the train, various children went in to meet the great man and seemed genuinely thrilled. They would emerge saying, 'I met Michael Jackson, I met Michael Jackson!'

We did meet Jackson ourselves, briefly. I shook his hand, and it was just like holding a crocodile

Steve Flack in the thick of it against Southend.

skin handbag – very dry and very soft. Ironically, given the incident with the cameraman, he wasn't wearing a glove. I was fixated on his nose, thinking, I hope it's not going to fall off. It looked so brittle.

Uri Geller took a picture of Jackson and me in the corridor of the train. I still have it on display in my house, as a reminder of a surreal day. The sign for the toilets is in between us.

They were truly three of the most eccentric characters in showbusiness, but my overriding impression of Michael Jackson was what a really nice guy he was. There was no arrogance; he was like the calm at the centre of the storm. It was rather like Pavarotti: while all this madness was going on, he was serene.

A Player's View

Steve Flack is an Exeter City legend. The usual shorthand for the 6ft 2in striker was 'ex-boxer', not least because it was true, but although he is an imposing figure, the nickname does scant justice to the skills which made the £10,000 City handed over to Cardiff City for his services in 1996 one of the club's shrewdest investments.

'Flacky' played for the club for 10 years, earning a richly deserved testimonial against Torquay on the way, and became only the third player to score in five consecutive Football League games for City.

A cult figure, Flack took the good-natured comments about his robust style in good part and scored 92 goals for City. It was his misfortune to play through some of the club's darkest days but his loyalty was never in doubt and he resisted several opportunities to move on, when the likes of Oxford, Hull, Bristol Rovers and Grimsby were prepared to pay up to £250,000 for his towering presence.

He still lives in East Devon, but during the 2002/03 season, as representative of the players' union, the PFA, he witnessed the financial crisis at the closest possible quarters and spent a good deal more time with Messrs Russell and Lewis than anyone would have wished.

'For a while I was in there nearly every other week about the wages not being paid,' he said. 'It was chaos: KFC boxes chucked under their desks in the boardroom – that's all they seemed to live on. I said that if there was no continuity off the pitch, they wouldn't get it on the pitch. Players were only earning an average man's wage – £600 to £700 a week – and they were worried about their mortgages and couldn't settle on the pitch. Russell said that he would guarantee, as long as he was chairman of the club, that the players would get their wages. A few months down the line we weren't getting paid and he got all the players together and said the same thing, but it was just a lot of words really.

'When the PFA subs came up, normal clubs deducted it from players' wages, but we couldn't trust Lewis and Russell to do it and the PFA said they'd accept cheques from the players. When Uri Geller was on *I'm a Celebrity* wearing his City shirt, he said he was the owner, but we found out later that he hadn't put any money in, they were just using his name.'

Not that there was no money around the club. 'Lee Sharpe was paid in cash after games,' Flack said, 'fifteen hundred to two grand a time. I once saw Sally Cooke, the club secretary at the time, leaving with a really heavy Tesco bag. I asked her what was in it and she said it was her wages – they had paid her in pound coins out of the fruit machine.

'It had gone on for years. Directors had put a minimum amount of money in and had been going to every away game for years, staying in the hotels,

even claiming expenses when they moved house. If you were a supporter you'd have paid that amount yourself to watch. There were too many people draining too much out of the club.'

Exeter's financial predicament earned Flack a moment of national exposure on the BBC's comedy sports quiz *They Think It's all Over*. The players had not been paid that month, and when he scored a goal in an away game Flack metaphorically 'passed the hat' to travelling City supporters. He was booked for his trouble.

'Finances dictate how football clubs look after you. I was one of the lucky ones – I got paid all the way through, even though some of it was late – but I know people who were owed thousands. If you are worth something to the club, they look after you, but if not . . . That's the reality of lower league football.'

The writing was probably on the wall for City's playing fortunes by October 2002 when the popular John Cornforth was sacked as manager and replaced by Neil McNab. When the new man turned to introduce his assistant, Gary Bennett, he couldn't remember his name. 'They even got that arse about face,' Flack recalled. 'They had given the assistant a job first and then looked for a manager without knowing whether they could work together or not.'

When Russell and Lewis wound up in court, Flack said they got little sympathy from the players. 'Life's a good leveller. They tried to get away with all sorts. When I asked if they would put £50 into the pot for the players' Christmas night out for drinks, they just handed me the club credit card.'

So, let's get this straight, Steve. When the club went bust owing millions of pounds, part of it was for the drinks bill for the players' night out in Torquay?

'Well, yes, but we did only spend about £200.'

Almost as soon as Exeter slipped out of the Football League, Neil McNab's successor as manager, Gary Peters, made it clear he would not be returning, and on 14 May, just 11 days after relegation was confirmed, Russell, Lewis and Russell's wife Gillian were arrested. It later emerged that Uri Geller was one of the people who had contacted the police to voice misgivings. The big question was not so much where Exeter would kick off the new season in the Conference but whether there would be a club at all.

CHAPTER TWO Can We Have Our Football Club Back, Please?

Comedian Adrian Edmondson spent the Southend game balanced precariously in a supermarket trolley in a garden behind the away end. Dean Moxey, a first-year professional who was to have a prominent part to play in Exeter's immediate history on the pitch, was collecting the supporters' money at the St James Road end. David Treharne and Julian Tagg were also in the ground, but in their cases the call to action sounded virtually when the referee blew the final whistle on Exeter City's membership of the Football League.

Football clubs get into debt, that much is obvious. But what happens when the debt is so mountainous, so overwhelming, that it is difficult to know where to start clearing it, never mind finish the job? This was what faced those brave souls who decided that if they didn't attempt to save Exeter City, no one else would.

Call to Arms: Part I

David Treharne, a history lecturer at the university, had a similar experience to many at the Southend game. 'Numbness really, although I first had to remove someone physically from my seat, for which I had a season ticket. My main feeling was that I might have witnessed the last ever game at St James Park.'

If it is true that the darkest hour is just before dawn, the glimmer of light which suggested that Exeter's position wasn't entirely hopeless had already been lit with the birth, in 2000, of the Supporters' Trust, which had endured an uneasy relationship with the club.

In fact, it had been a year earlier, in 2002 and with 250 members, that the fans' agenda had changed radically. 'The Trust had taken the decision that the aim was no longer to support the club but to run the club, which was laughable,' Treharne said. 'During 2002/03 the membership grew steadily, to about 750 towards the end of the season, as a lot of the forebodings people had had were borne out by what they had seen going on. Dealing with Russell and Lewis was extraordinarily difficult. They kept telling us that, as amateurs, we couldn't possibly run a football club.

'However, we had messages of support from other clubs, and one person, who called himself Swansea Jack, provided an incredible amount of information about what had happened there [Lewis had sold the club for £1]. We also had a great ally in David Conn of *The Independent* who was absolutely fantastic. He kept in touch with us right through the season.'

David Conn is a journalist who specialises in exposing financial misdeeds in football. 'My brief is to champion good management at football clubs and I firmly believe they should all belong to their fans, not businessmen who want to make money out of buying them,' he said. 'Triumphantly, Exeter does belong to the fans now, but Russell and Lewis clearly conflicted with that ethos, so we got stuck into them.

'Somebody well connected in football tipped me off that John Russell had a conviction. I checked it out with the court and was stunned to discover that he could just walk into a football club. My article about him was news to the rest of the board at Exeter. Russell is the one person a fit and proper person test would have stopped.'

Russell was confronted about his conviction for obtaining property by deception in an infamous appearance on Adrian Durham's show on TalkSport radio, when the presenter's aggressive line of questioning appeared to catch him unawares. With impeccable logic, Russell blustered that 'It wasn't property, it was a JCB!'

'They did slag me off as well,' Conn added, 'saying I wouldn't know one end of a football from another. Which is quite true, given that it doesn't have one!'

The Trust may have been small, but it did have something the club wanted. 'Probably the best thing was that the Trust had decided not to support Russell and Lewis in any way with finance,' said Treharne. 'They knew we had money but we weren't prepared to hand it over.'

The arrest of Russell and Lewis was to prove a watershed. 'Ivor [Doble] had wanted out for a considerable time but he didn't have a Plan B,' said Treharne. 'He was relieved that Russell and Lewis were out of it and he approached Julian, Terry Pavey and Ian Huxham [chair of the Trust] about the possibility of running some sort of interim regime.'

Mike Lewis and John Russell watch events unfold on the pitch at St James Park.

Dr David Treharne.

Julian Tagg.

It is in the nature of a voluntary organisation such as the Trust that personalities change constantly as people dip in and out of the story, but Treharne identifies one constant in the story: Julian Tagg. 'Julian felt an attachment, though I don't think on his own he would have been able to put together a consortium to take over the club, and in many ways the other two provided complementary talents. Ian was a great motivator, and Terry [who spent much of the summer sleeping in a camper van outside St James Park], because he ran his own business, had a very solid idea of what would be needed in terms of putting in place an organisation simply to fill any hole that arrived – and, of course, the hole arrived as soon as the police arrested Russell and Lewis.

'That summer was horrific. We kept on having bailiffs round. A parking ticket in York which the management had neglected to pay started off at £30 and arrived at us at £250. We had the standby generator repossessed, and so on. The consensus was that unless we owned the club there was no point in trying to carry on. I have copies of two letters the Trust prepared at the time: one announcing that we were prepared to take over the club, and the other saying that as of 6 September the Trust would withdraw its support for the club. And we would have done – no two ways about it.

'I was deputed to negotiate with Ivor through a local firm of solicitors but he, as indeed did all the former directors, reckoned that the club had a value and there was a real question of what we would pay. I was authorised to go up to £30,000.'

If Treharne's negotiating position appeared unpromising, the backdrop to the negotiations was that membership of the Trust was soaring – a clear indication of a real will to succeed among supporters. The Trust might not have had much money, but they had the momentum.

'There was some real brinkmanship. We gave Ivor an ultimatum and then I was asked to be at Ivor's [jewellery] shop at 9.30 a.m. one day. He wanted the deal done that morning so I summoned my solicitor, Simon Armitage, and Ed Probert, who had done most of the legwork on the purchase, and got Martin Ellicott, a Trust member, to come over and witness the sale on behalf of the Trust.'

When he emerged from the shop, Treharne did so with a 63 per cent shareholding in the club. 'I really did wake up the next morning feeling euphoric that I'd bought the club for the Trust, and then thought, My God, three million pounds' debt

Scott Hiley, a City legend with more than 250 appearances.

– maybe. In fact it was a lot more than that. David Conn caught it really well in *The Independent* with his article headlined "Exeter Face the Coming Storm with Faith, Hope and Charity".'

Call to Arms: Part II

It is hardly surprising that Julian Tagg has the youth of Exeter City at heart. A ballboy when Manchester United played at St James Park in the FA Cup third round in 1968, he made his debut for the reserves as a 15-year-old, and although he was never taken on as an apprentice by City, he played for Exeter College, the county and St Luke's until, at the age of 23, a knee injury sustained in a car crash ended any hopes of carrying on playing seriously. After a break from football, he became involved with the game again in 1998 when his son, Toby, showed promise and City's youth coach, Mike Radford, suggested he form a team for some of the best up-and-coming players in the area.

When Russell and Lewis took £60,000 from the youth account, they set in train a process that would culminate in Tagg taking a central role in Exeter's history over the coming years. 'A friend of mine, Richard Hodgson, staked them out and got them to sign a letter that they had taken the money,' he said. 'It was a personal letter of guarantee. I don't know how much that piece of paper was worth but it was more than what was written on it.'

One other rather random incident acted as motivation. 'I was listening to David Fitzgerald's radio programme in the car and someone from Plymouth called in and said, "What's happening at Exeter City? They've got Michael Jackson, Uri Geller and Darth Vader – all they need now is Coco the Clown for the full set!" As so many people in Exeter were probably feeling at the time, we were embarrassed by what had been going on in the name of our club and our city.

'The reason I came on board in the first place [as an associate director] was because they were going to shut the youth down. I came to the ground with Ivor Doble the night before Russell and Lewis were arrested and put locks on the doors to keep them out because they hadn't paid any of the bills. I knew what was going on because the money had gone and I knew there was a problem. I put my neck on the line – although I didn't realise how badly on the line it was because I didn't know the level of the debt; I hadn't a clue it was £4.8 million, though I knew it was a couple of million – because I didn't want the youth department to close.'

A Club Worth Saving?

Relegation marked the lowest point in Exeter City's history, and the debts were on an unprecedented, eye-watering scale, but no one could pretend that the club had not flirted with demotion and bankruptcy before.

By 2003, Terry Cooper's Fourth Division title-winning team of 1990 seemed a long way off. In the intervening years, City had slipped back into the bottom division in 1994, lost ownership of the ground, and finished bottom of the entire Football League in 1995, only surviving relegation to the Conference because the ground of Macclesfield, who were due to travel in the opposite direction as champions, was deemed unfit for what had by now been renamed Division Three.

One can only hazard a guess at the reaction of Sir Alan Sugar, or the gurus from *Dragons' Den*, had they been presented with City's business plans for the future.

And yet, despite a great deal of mediocre football and almost annual trips to the FA to explain away a perennially dreadful disciplinary record, whenever City made it to the upper echelons of the division they were in or drew notable opponents in the FA or League Cups, interest soared.

Exeter's history is one of modest achievement combined with a happy knack of unearthing strikers who scored at a prodigious rate. Alan Banks, a Liverpudlian, starred in the promotion team of 1964, and Alan Beer and Tony Kellow were an irresistible pairing in the 1977 promotion team under John Newman.

The last time Exeter really made national headlines for the right reasons was under Brian Godfrey, a dour Welshman who managed in the space of a year to achieve the club's best League finish – eighth in Division Three in 1980 – and then led the club to the quarter-finals of the FA Cup, a run during which they were invariably referred to in the national press as 'little' Exeter. For supporters of a certain age, it was memories of these more glorious times that sustained them through much of the disappointment that followed.

City's 1981 Cup run is the stuff of legend. After beating Leatherhead, Millwall and Maidstone, they travelled to Leicester – struggling, but in the top division – and earned a 1–1 draw. The Exeter City team was vastly experienced, with Len Bond in goal, Phil Roberts at centre-half, John Delve in midfield and Cornishman Kellow leading the attack. It was no great surprise when they beat Leicester 3–1 amid tumultuous scenes at St James Park, in what was arguably Kellow's finest hour and a half: he scored a hat-trick, including a penalty which raged past goalkeeper Mark Wallington and into the top left-hand corner and which, he maintains, was the best strike of a football in his illustrious career.

Then, as now, Newcastle were enduring a torrid time and were only one division above City. Nonetheless a trip to the 'other' St James' Park in the fifth round was still a daunting prospect, but again City came away with a replay, defender Lee Roberts (no relation to Phil) hooking the ball in from close range in the dying minutes to secure a 1–1 draw.

On the face of it, 'Where do Exeter City play?' is not the most taxing question, but the spelling of the answer has taxed signwriters, journalists and anyone who gives a fig about punctuation down the ages.

For perfectly sound reasons, and with admirable consistency, the *Express and Echo* sticks doggedly with St James's Park, like the one in London: it is the Park of St James, after all. The club programme takes an even-handed view, using St James Park, St James' Park and St James's Park virtually interchangeably.

The sign outside the Old Grandstand used to boast a dangling apostrophe (St James' Park), but when it was repainted the apostrophe disappeared. Quite right, too. St James' Park is in Newcastle. Why it is there (the apostrophe that is, not Newcastle) nobody knows, but the fact that two clubs have very similar names for their grounds has been enough to confuse *Daily Telegraph* sports sub-editors for as long as anyone can remember.

The people running the club have had more important things to worry about than punctuation, but because St James Road is next to the ground, and to save ink, this book has gone with St James Park. This is not a definitive ruling, but a little consistency wouldn't hurt.

To anyone who thinks punctuation doesn't matter, here is an illuminating story, which is not apocryphal (after all, no one could make it up). In the dim and distant past, London-based City fans found, to their delight and astonishment, that they could travel from London Paddington to St James Park (Exeter) for the price of a £1.50 Tube ticket to St James's Park (Westminster) – a saving of £43.50, and a sure sign of a benevolent higher being, given the quality of the football on offer at SJP at the time.

Tony Kellow, Exeter's record goalscorer.

Promotion-winning manager Terry Cooper and his son and goalscoring midfielder, Mark.

The replay, on 18 February, was a fairytale. A total of 17,668 fans squeezed into the Park, plus John Motson, who climbed the ladder (yes, really) to the commentary gantry in the Cowshed so that he could tell the country all about the match on that evening's *Sportsnight.* And what a story he had to tell. Newcastle may have been a poor team, but City dismantled them and had the game won by half-time, when they led 3–0 thanks to goals from Peter Hatch, Ian Pearson (a spectacular overhead kick) and Peter Rogers. Defender Martyn Rogers, Peter's cousin, added a fourth, but by then City knew they were on their way to White Hart Lane for the quarter-finals.

St James Park, City's home since 1904.

Rebuilding work and filthy weather made the trip to Tottenham a little less glamorous than it might otherwise have been, and although City gave an enormously creditable performance in front of 40,629 fans, goals from defenders Graham Roberts and Paul Miller ended that particular dream and two months later Spurs captain Steve Perryman lifted the Cup at Wembley after an epic replay victory over Manchester City. (I wonder, whatever happened to him?)

Three years after that quarter-final, City went down to the Fourth Division, despite the presence of former England captain Gerry Francis in the dugout. It would be six years before City returned to the third tier when Terry Cooper, shrewdly moulding a combination of experienced players such as Clive Whitehead and Steve Neville with promising youngsters including Kevin Miller, Scott Hiley and Richard Dryden, stormed to the Fourth Division title. Another striker had been unearthed in Darran Rowbotham, who topped the goalscoring charts but missed out on a move to Chelsea after suffering a terrible cruciate ligament knee injury.

City survived at the higher level for four years, but the departure of manager Alan Ball for Southampton early in 1994 signalled the beginning of the end and the club slipped lamely back into Division Four. No one, even in their worst nightmare, could have imagined it would be 15 years before they returned.

Brazil Masters line up before kick off.

Exeter City began their first season outside the Football League with a home game against Halifax Town. They ended it with a match against Brazil. Now what does that say about the club's ambition and refusal to let a little thing like millions of pounds of debt wipe them off the football map?

The easiest thing in the world after relegation, recrimination and virtual extinction would have been to put any sort of celebration on hold. Instead, on 30 May 2004, City marked their centenary with a game against the Brazil Masters, six of whom had been part of the World Cup-winning team in the United States 10 years earlier. When it finally noticed what was going on down in Devon, the world was agog. What on earth was Branco, recently of Middlesbrough, doing in charge of a team containing Dunga, Jorginho and Careca? More to the point, why did this collection of supremely gifted South Americans keep talking about what a privilege it was to be playing a no-hope team from the Conference? And how come Exeter officials had attended a reception hosted by the Brazilian ambassador in London to greet the team's arrival?

The story took quite a lot of believing, but in 1914, when England was still regarded as the guardian of the game and there was no such thing as professional football in Brazil, the authorities, when asked to send a 'typically English' club to

help promote the game in the continent, nominated Exeter City, of the Southern League.

It was to prove a lively trip. A cultural misunderstanding soon led to the team falling foul of the law: when the squad trained on the beach in Santos they were arrested for bathing without their tops on, though they were soon released without charge. Exeter won a couple of games, then on 21 July at Fluminese's ground they met a Brazil team made up of players from both Rio and São Paulo – now regarded as Brazil's first truly 'national' team. ('I've done my homework,' Branco said. 'I started my career at Fluminese, so I have the connections.') A crowd of 6,000 packed the small ground and went delirious with excitement when Brazil opened the scoring in the first half. It was a heated occasion – two Exeter players left the pitch temporarily in protest at some of the referee's decisions. A second Brazil goal soon followed, and that was how the score remained, 2–0 – Brazil's first victory.

It would be fair to say that events in Exeter 90 years on were a little less heated, one over-zealous tackle in the second half excepted. Ironically, Exeter's Brazilian defender, Santos Gaia, was back in his homeland, and the hosts took the wise precaution of playing an extremely young team and changing most of them at half-time. This didn't stop the veterans from Brazil enjoying what seemed to be about 80 per cent of the possession. Careca's passport may have said 44, but his movement off the ball was startling, while Silas's step-overs on the left wing mesmerised fans and opponents alike.

Careca scored the only goal, from the penalty spot, just before half-time, but really this was a lesson in the finer arts of the game. Glenn Cronin, the Exeter captain, was impressed. 'They just kept the ball for fun, showed us how to play. Dunga walked through the whole game. Unbelievable.'

For Steve Flack, who did not habitually play to a samba beat, it was also a memorable day. 'After the game we had a meal at the Devon Hotel and Dunga said we were the first club team they had played. It was a good day and a good evening.

'At Exeter, some players thought they were great, but Brazil were in their forties and in a different class. Those sorts of players are born with instinct to know where to be. You can't be taught to be that good and we ran around after the ball. They were talking through the game, demanding stuff off their own players and a bit of shouting if they did something wrong. It was a great experience.'

It was all marvellously incongruous, especially when a feverish pocket of Brazilians and wannabe Brazilians pummelled their drums, blew their whistles, flourished flags and sang and danced in one of the ground's more dingy corners.

'This club has been kept afloat by people who have donated out of the goodness of their hearts,' said Ian Huxham. It has to be said that some were aghast at being asked to pay up to £30 for a ticket to the festivities, but the 6,000 crowd, enlivened by a few typically colourful Brazil natives and a large samba troupe, ensured Exeter made a profit.

If the game reaffirmed the Brazilians' affinity for our national game, it also said something pertinent about Exeter City: we are still here, so don't write us off yet.

Hand to Mouth

The club had made it to the end of that 2003/04 season but it had not been easy. The story had been as much about debt off the pitch as points on it; of administration, transfer embargoes, the threat of a points deductions, of a growing number of Trust members (who could join for a few pounds a month to help keep the club afloat), and of the innovative Red or Dead campaign in which 350 ordinary fans pledged £500 each to help the club pay its debts.

In football, normal rules don't apply. Exeter's

A Brazilian beat at the Park.

Branco, manager of the Brazil team.

supporters found themselves on the horns of a classic dilemma. To save the club, they had to enter a CVA (Company Voluntary Arrangement) in October with their non-football creditors, which meant companies accepting a fraction of the combined £3,196,616 they were owed rather than see the club go bust and risk getting nothing. The Inland Revenue, owed £233,000, voted against.

However, football rules mean that 'football creditors' – i.e. managers, players and other clubs – get everything that they are owed. And they get it first, while the local piemen and programme printers receive a few pence in the pound.

Exeter's supporters could argue, just as Luton fans would find a few years later, that they were merely clearing up a mess left by someone else. The Conference took a different view and threatened to dock City 12 points for going into administration, as well as an obligatory transfer embargo. When the supporters who had rescued the club from oblivion most wanted help, they

Dunga in complete control.

The Pressure Mounts

David Treharne recalls an agonising, draining period in the club's history. 'I felt desperately sorry for John Cornforth, who had been sacked as manager and didn't want the club to go into CVA. It was a very difficult time.

'Almost as soon as we bought the club we decided that we would have to go into CVA. As we were individuals who were liable for the debt we got as many people onto the board as possible. Geoffrey Styles, as company secretary, Roger Monksummers, Roger Hamilton-Kendall, from the supporters' club, and Barry Sansom. Jerry O'Sullivan, who was appointed as supervisor of the CVA, and others – including an honourable mention for Ben Bradshaw, Exeter's MP – set about trying to make people who were owed money agree, and it was no mean feat. It certainly looked as though Mowlem's, the builders, weren't keen, and it was a pretty close-run thing. You have to have a meeting of the creditors and a majority have to agree. When you looked down the list of creditors there were a surprising number of laundrettes. As laundrettes refused to give the old regime any more credit, they had simply moved on to another. Another major one was the brewery. Damned frightening it was, and something to be ashamed of, because it was full of businesses who could ill afford to lose money. The meeting was not pleasant. In the end the creditors got 7.2 pence in the pound.'

found themselves pursued on all sides. A major adversary was the Inland Revenue, which challenged the validity of the CVA because it did not get the preferred status of football creditors.

Stephen Allinson, the club's insolvency expert, said that City had no choice but to go on the attack and make theirs a test case for the game. 'It is just unfortunate that Exeter City are having to do it and not a big club like Leeds United,' he lamented.

When City, benefiting from some free legal help, sued the Conference for 'unfairly prejudicial' treatment in an attempt to clarify their position, the Conference told other clubs it could cost them £25,000 each to defend the High Court action. For a time it seemed City were the most hated club in the land, with some rivals demanding they be expelled.

At one point, when the Conference, perhaps rather conveniently, ruled that City's signing of midfielder Dwayne Lee had broken their rules by taking place after a transfer embargo came into force, the club was faced with the prospect of a 36-point deduction and almost certain relegation.

In the end, some sort of common sense prevailed. Tony Kleanthous, the Barnet chairman, weighed in on City's behalf at several meetings of the board of the Conference and played a major role in staving off a points deduction. When the Football Association put pressure on them to back down, the Conference agreed to drop the threat of a points deduction and City soldiered on, although football creditors retained their protected status.

Fire-fighting

Doing deals was the only way to reduce the club's debt, which meant negotiating with companies and players, many of whom had left months earlier. It is at times like these that the football seems almost an afterthought. Julian Tagg and Steve Flack had regular meetings to work out how City were going to have enough bodies even to field a team. 'I was very aware that you are responsible for somebody else's problem and you have to clean up the mess,' Tagg said, 'and to make decisions that affect people's mortgages, homes and everything else.

'Footballers were protected to a certain extent, because of the preferential creditor rule, but many were not being paid before we arrived and thought the club was going downhill and wanted to go. Anybody who wanted to come off the wage bill, did. There was a transfer embargo, so you couldn't bring people in, you just had to get on with what you had and make sure you had enough people to

World Cup-winning captain Dunga puts Gareth Sheldon in his place.

Dunga tries on Glenn Cronin's Exeter shirt for size.

put on the pitch. The trouble was that some were on contracts commensurate with League One or Two, and we were skint. Even today, nobody is on the money Sean Devine was on then. It was a phenomenal contract. Phenomenal. Way beyond anything today.'

Justin Quick, a recent recruit from accountants Bishop Fleming, joined Tagg to negotiate, cajole or otherwise persuade former players and other clubs to come to an arrangement. 'Because of the football creditors rule, you have to pay in full in order to stay in football. Basically it was a case of picking up the phone and asking people, one by one, whether they wanted the money now or in staged payments. Some were very helpful and there are some real unsung heroes that were great to the club, but some were particularly difficult. They demanded payment in full, which they are quite entitled to do. Other clubs were sympathetic, but they all need every penny to spend on players. The bigger the club, the more receptive they were likely to be.'

Green Shoots

Although the cash flow was dreadful, the atmosphere around the club was transformed. Over the summer, an enormous amount of work was done at the ground by fans in return for nothing but the satisfaction of doing it and a cup of tea.

There were other acts of kindness, such as one from City's closest rivals. 'Mike Bateson, the Torquay chairman, agreed to play a friendly simply

to help us get some cash and then forfeited their share of the gate – several thousand pounds,' said Treharne.

The board, none of whom was being paid or taking expenses, did their best to staunch the flow of cash out of the club. 'We held weekly board meetings to address the dire financial situation. I became chair of the club because it was felt that no one person should hold the roles of both chair and managing director. The thing that amazed us was that companies like Bartlett Refrigeration, who had no right to touch us with a bargepole, not only continued to trade with us but gave us advantageous deals. So many of the businesses around Exeter that had been really quite hurt stood by the club.

'That first season was an extraordinary learning curve. We didn't really know anything at all about what went on behind the scenes. It wasn't always possible for more than one director to get to away games. Other clubs expected you to be there in force, even if it was only to give you an ear bashing to tell you how lucky you were to still have a club. I remember having a conversation at Accrington with Eric Whalley, their chairman, and him telling me it was disgusting that we were still in business when Accrington had gone bust in the sixties owing about £30,000.'

Not for the first time, the club would have to adapt to changing circumstances, and steps were taken to reorganise the board. 'Jerry [O'Sullivan] persuaded us to appoint someone to run the club, which was a major mistake, because Ian Huxham

Eamonn Dolan.

Sean Devine is consoled by his wife after City miss out on the play-offs.

was appointed to run the club on a salary which we couldn't afford.

'There were too many directors, and Geoffrey Styles was running a business in Germany, which was impractical. We needed a group of people to meet on a regular basis at short notice. I had no pleasure in doing it but we got rid of Geoffrey as company secretary, which retrospectively was done very badly. Is there a good way? I don't know, but I was the guy who did it.'

There were also signs of a lack of appreciation of their efforts among the supporters. 'Having got hold of the club there was a fairly high level of personal abuse from some supporters, who were saying, "You're not doing this very well." If anyone tells you it was a smooth path that's completely erroneous. We made some horrendous mistakes.'

Meanwhile, on the Pitch.....

Despite the prospect of a skeleton squad and a transfer embargo, former City striker Eamonn Dolan stepped up from the youth department to take the manager's job and the club's star striker – 'Sean Devine, Devine, he wears number ten not

nine' – went a long way to justifying his enormous salary with 25 goals.

Dolan is credited with eradicating a booze culture among some of his players, but not before an outburst after a 1–0 home defeat by Gravesend in February, when he said that two players had been out drinking during the week before the game. 'My message is "go and be a pub player – don't play for Exeter City". We got relegated last year because it was an alcohol club – that's why, no other reason.'

In the end, City finished sixth. A remarkable crowd of 8,256 turned up for the final home game, against Accrington, to see if they could make it into the end-of-season play-offs. City won 3–2 but missed out, by just one point. Getting out of the Conference was clearly not going to be easy.

It may have seemed a parochial concern in the wider context of the club's battle for survival but, to rub salt into the wound, the next season the Grecians would not only be playing three divisions below Plymouth Argyle but two below Torquay. All three Devon clubs had been in the same division as recently as 2002.

Spend a few minutes in Steve Perryman's company and an insatiable love of football reverberates around the room – a detailed demonstration of why Tottenham's David Bentley was standing in the wrong place when defending a post at a corner, for instance. There's a fund of stories too.

If a name occasionally escapes him, Perryman can be forgiven the odd pause, given the size of his contacts book. He played 654 times for Tottenham in 19 years at the club, winning a solitary England cap along the way (seven minutes as a substitute against Iceland in the build-up to the 1982 World Cup, when he had just been voted Player of the Year by the Football Writers) – a poor return for almost two decades of consistency, predominantly in midfield but also at right-back. Famously, he lifted the FA Cup twice as captain in successive years, 1981 and 1982, although he endured a torrid return to Tottenham as assistant manager to Ossie Ardiles. The perceived wisdom is that the Spurs team that began the 1994/95 season, featuring Jurgen Klinsmann, Teddy Sheringham, Nick Barmby and Ilie Dumitrescu, was wonderful going forward but incompetent at the back, which must have wounded this stalwart of the Tottenham defence. 'Sacked and slaughtered', in Perryman's words, the pair headed for Japan where he rediscovered his love of football. Even after Ardiles left, Perryman guided Shimzu S-Pulse to the Championship and Asian Cup Winners' Cup.

Exeter's training ground, the Cat & Fiddle, must have seemed a long way off, but when Noel Blake was struggling to keep City in the Football League in 2001 Perryman pitched in, at the invitation of City director Joe Gadston, and helped the Christian Roberts-inspired Grecians to stave off disaster – for the time being at least.

Perryman missed the Russell and Lewis era but arrived as director of football in the immediate aftermath of relegation to the Conference, again at Gadston's instigation. 'He had been my youth coach when I was Brentford manager, but when he asked me, I just said, "Joe, why?" He said, "Well, I'm here and I really believe we can make players here." I wasn't convinced, but eventually he wore me down.

'The club couldn't have gone any lower without folding and it was the start of the good times, I suppose,' he reflected, with a surprising

Steve Perryman.

Alex Inglethorpe.

enthusiasm for a club which was in a predicament so dire it might have prompted others to take the first train back to London.

Perryman has played his considerable part, helping a succession of rookie managers with his knowledge and unquenchable enthusiasm. He worked for nothing for three years. Not that he regards the gift of his time as unreciprocated. 'I was lucky to have had a good career and been successful as a manager in Japan. But when I came back, after seven years, London disappointed me. After a season helping from afar, with two young daughters, Exeter seemed an ideal place to relocate. It was out of the mainstream and Ossie said I must be mad. I told him about the lovely countryside and the slower pace of life, but it took a while to get him down to Lympstone.'

Until the summer of 2009, the only way most national newspaper sports editors could be persuaded to show any interest in Exeter was to be invited to hang it on the peg of 'Spurs legend slums it in Devon'. The reality, of course, was rather different, as the unashamedly old-school Perryman lent his considerable expertise to help Eamonn Dolan, Alex Inglethorpe and, latterly, Paul Tisdale stabilise and then improve the playing side of the club, while on match days he could be heard bellowing support to the players from the Old Grandstand. 'I have experience to give but I am learning about the scientific approach, the testing, from intelligent young managers. I like a lot of it but there is also a place for the old-fashioned way as well.'

As Perryman put it in the build-up to Exeter's trip to Wembley to play Morecambe in 2007, with typically infectious enthusiasm, 'It has been a great ride, a terrific story. Exeter deserves League football – the crowds tell you that. People have put themselves on the line for that club. It may not be good enough on the pitch on Sunday, but it's not the old Exeter. This is everyone pulling in the same direction, and eventually it will bear fruit.'

All Change in the Dugout

Early in the 2004/05 season, Eamonn Dolan received an offer to take charge of Reading's youth academy which proved irresistible. Steve Perryman and veteran defender Scott Hiley took charge temporarily until City appointed Alex Inglethorpe, although not before a hilarious story linking Plymouth's Paul Sturrock with the job. Sturrock had come to watch two players Plymouth had loaned City, at a very advantageous rate, and sat alongside Julian Tagg at the game. A picture and wildly improbable story appeared in the local press before anyone worked out the implausibility of Exeter being able to afford the Scot.

Although Inglethorpe, an attacking midfielder, had played for City in the 2000/01 season, scoring a couple of goals in 19 appearances, of more relevance was his spell in charge of Leatherhead and his most recent job, as Leyton Orient's under-19s coach. He was a few weeks short of his 33rd birthday – scant experience for the national prominence he was to enjoy within three months of taking the job.

The Great FA Cup Adventure

As a Conference team, Exeter joined the FA Cup at the fourth qualifying stage, a round earlier than the Football League teams – one more reason why

Steve Flack powers in to score against Doncaster.

Steve Flack and Dean Moxey, goalscorers against Doncaster.

Teenage goalkeeper Paul Jones prepares to step into the limelight.

there was little prospect of a meeting with glamorous opposition, even after City beat Braintree Town 2–0 at home.

But then Grimsby, from League Two, were seen off 1–0, and Doncaster Rovers arrived for a second-round tie on 4 December. Off the field, enormous efforts had been made to stabilise the club's fortunes; this game can be seen as the catalyst to proving that the players could match the efforts of the supporters.

Doncaster were a prime example of how a club can be reborn. They had slipped out of the League in ignominy in 1998 and their former owner, Ken Richardson, had been jailed for having the grandstand at the hugely inappropriately named Belle Vue burned down in an effort to claim the insurance money. Doncaster had enjoyed the benefit of a wealthy benefactor in John Ryan, but they were currently two divisions above City and had James Coppinger, one of the best players of recent years in red and white, on the bench. It looked a mighty tall order.

However, in a sign of what was to come in the third round, City set about Rovers with a vengeance. Midway through the first half, Steve Flack flattened goalkeeper Andy Warrington as he made thunderous contact with Alex Jeannin's perfectly flighted free kick to seize the lead.

Meanwhile, the experienced Kwame Ampadu had limped off and City had unleashed 18-year-old Dean Moxey from the bench for a hyperactive performance that would probably have earned him the man of the match award even without the mighty 45-yard shot which dipped under Warrington's crossbar. Some of Moxey's team-mates had their doubts about how intentional this

wonder goal was. Flack, perhaps rather uncharitably, said, 'He tried to hit Sean Devine. You can see him look up. He caught it sweet enough and it just managed to go in underneath the crossbar with the keeper backtracking, but sometimes you need that bit of luck to win games.' The goal gave City the insurance they needed to survive a barrage of late Doncaster pressure and make it into the hat for the third round.

Things were looking up.

And Now, at FA Headquarters in Soho Square.....

The name Tony Cascarino had barely figured in the history of Exeter City until a fateful afternoon in December 2004. History may well show that in pairing City's number 64 ball with Manchester United's during the FA Cup third round draw, he helped save the club. Certainly at the time it seemed that between them Cascarino and Dean Moxey could have found an improbable route to salvation after two bleak years.

A television crew captured the wonderful sight of Steve Perryman dancing around his sitting room like a teenager with Alex Inglethorpe. This was more than a football match, this was light at the end of the longest, bleakest financial tunnel anyone could imagine. So amid the excitement of organising a 10,000-strong exodus from Devon to the Theatre of Dreams, it was reassuring that Exeter retained a sense of perspective.

The obvious newspaper story was that here was the real hope of a happy ending for the supporters who were not prepared to watch their club die, but managing director Ian Huxham was eager to dispel the notion that one game at Old Trafford, even one

Steve Perryman and Alex Inglethorpe hear the FA Cup draw.

producing a £600,000 payday, would end Exeter's worries. 'We didn't start from zero, we started from minus,' he said. 'It is not enough to build the football club our supporters deserve.'

What Huxham could not imagine, nor anyone else for that matter, was that there would be two games against Manchester United, live television coverage from St James Park of Cristiano Ronaldo, Wayne Rooney et al, and the biggest and most positive headlines City had enjoyed for a generation.

Old Trafford – The Dream Turns into Reality

Manchester United 0 Exeter City 0

Manchester United: Howard; P. Neville, Pique, Brown, Spector; Eagles (Ronaldo 63), Miller (Scholes 63), Djemba-Djemba, D. Jones; Richardson, Bellion (Smith 75).
Subs: Ricardo (g), Heinze

Exeter City: P. Jones; Hiley, Gaia, Sawyer, Jeannin; Taylor (Edwards 88), Clay (Ampadu 65), Martin, Moxey; Flack (Afful 74), Devine.
Subs: Rice (g), Sheldon

Referee: P. Dowd

Attendance: 67,551

And then, one month later, 10,000 Devonians and

a dozen Norwegians from the further outpost of the Supporters' Club woke up having dreamt that Exeter City, of the Nationwide Conference, had been to the Theatre of Dreams and held mighty Manchester United to a goalless draw in the FA Cup.

They came by bus, train and plane – although, given the speed of some, the combine harvesters honoured in several club songs would have been as quick – and the smiles were scarcely any broader after this eye-rubbing result than before.

If Manchester United weren't very good it was because 14 Exeter players gave everything they had, to prove that there is life in a club that might have quietly expired several times in the past couple of years. That day was about affirmation that Exeter City, despite a mountain of problems, could and would survive. A reward for the hundreds of 'Red or Dead' fans who'd pledged £500 each to help repay the club's debts; for legendary goalscorer Alan Banks, who was in the crowd; and for Dean Moxey and Andy Taylor, Exeter-born, Manchester United-supporting players who excelled on the pitch.

This was publicity for the right reason. Not Uri Geller wearing a City shirt on *I'm a Celebrity Get Me Out of Here*, or Michael Jackson making a personal appearance at St James Park, or

A young fan in position early at Old Trafford.

City's players form a huddle.

Andy Taylor lets fly.

outlandish bids to put a clearly declining Gazza in charge. Dreams that turned to dust with relegation from the Football League. As one fan gloomily admitted, Exeter fans did not regard themselves as non-League, but the rest of the world did. Technically, the world had a point.

Out on the pitch, United had a World Cup player,

Eric Djemba-Djemba, but City boasted a goalscoring Brazilian centre-half in Santos Gaia. Swap? No thanks. United were missing Ruud van Nistelrooy, but City captain Glenn Cronin was out for the season. United were playing some youngsters, but City goalkeeper Paul Jones – an inspired signing by Alex Inglethorpe from Leyton

Paul Jones denies Paul Scholes.

Steve Flack powers on through the deluge.

The scoreline that shook the world.

Orient's youth team – was starting his third senior game. At 18.

From the top of the East Stand, Exeter fans received news from home (the fishmonger's had closed early because the city was deserted) and questioned the status of the United team (just who was Gerard Pique anyway?). But this was surely a phoney war, the prelude to a very sound thrashing to accompany a very large cheque. Club saved; mission accomplished.

What unfolded still seems surreal. Jones, who really looked a player, made a couple of early saves before Taylor hammered a 20-yarder straight at Tim Howard (a yard or two either way . . .). Some thought Phil Neville handled in the area, and then Taylor rippled the outside of the net with an almost perfect free kick.

Half-time. Surely Sir Alex Ferguson hadn't expected this, and Cristiano Ronaldo, Paul Scholes and Alan Smith would be off the bench for the second half. In the meantime, 10,000 voices extolled the virtues of cider and roundly abused Plymouth Argyle. A curiously moving experience.

The big guns arrived, eventually, and with 20

Andy Gillard's phones in the commercial department are red hot before the replay.

One of the country's top young talents and Cristiano Ronaldo battle for possession.

Paul Scholes proves elusive.

minutes left Exeter's 8-2 formation looked ominous. Steve Flack, the towering ex-boxer, could barely move. Sean Devine was running through treacle. But they kicked on and got lucky when Scholes missed with virtually the last kick.

Financially, Exeter undoubtedly benefited from United's less-than-total commitment to the FA Cup and the willingness of United supporters to pay to watch 11 red shirts drying in the breeze to put some black into the bank account to match their black centenary shirts, but there were four England internationals on the pitch at the end.

The FA Cup can still remind more exalted supporters that there is life beyond the rarefied world of the Champions League. As Paul, from Exeter, said, 'A lot of people I met on the tram didn't know where Devon was, let alone what league Exeter are in. I had to explain what the Conference is.'

For Steve Flack, the experience of playing United could not have been sweeter. 'My missus has watched me play on a rec with two people and their dog watching, pissing down with rain and a bucket of water for first aid. So it was nice, 13 or 14 years down the line, to be playing at one of the best stadiums in the world against some of the best players in the world.

'When I got there I just wanted to spend as much time as I could on the pitch, get changed and absorb a once-in-a-lifetime experience. We had to play the best we could play and they had to have an average to poor game for us to stand any sort of chance, but we had a couple of moments when they had a little heart murmur.

'When you play you don't take much notice of who is there to watch, because you are so

shattered, but the City fans were fantastic. Alex Ferguson said it was Exeter's day and all about them, and it put a bit of romance back into the FA Cup.

'I think the Man United game catapulted the club forward three or four years. Without it, they might still be in the Conference trying to piece it together.'

Midfielder Andy Taylor, who had turned out for nothing for City during the transfer embargo, fulfilled a lifelong ambition by playing at Old Trafford. He had spent three years with United before suffering a serious knee injury and being released. Injury had also cost him the chance of appearing for United there in an FA Youth Cup tie, so it was an auspicious day. 'Sir Alex Ferguson made himself known to me and asked how I was getting on and wished me good luck in everything, which was nice.

'My free kick didn't quite go in – that would have really capped off the day. But it was still a brilliant occasion. The highlight of my career? Well, it's the

Sir Alex Ferguson in the St James Park technical area.

Santos Gaia keeps tabs on Wayne Rooney.

one the fans always talk about, so I would have to say yes.'

For David Treharne and the rest of the board, the experience was both tinged with unreality and a reward for months of toil. 'The club and the directors had a lot to be proud of in what they had achieved. We had a fantastic, fantastic day. And flying back to Exeter and being met by a huge group of people – even if they didn't want to see me – was a fantastic feeling.'

One Night in Devon

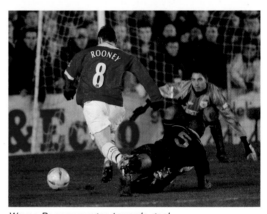
Wayne Rooney surges towards goal.

Exeter City 0 Manchester United 2 (Ronaldo 9, Rooney 87)

Exeter City: Jones; Hiley, Gaia, Sawyer, Jeannin; Taylor (Martin 86), Clay, Ampadu (Afful 67), Moxey; Flack (Edwards 73), Devine.
Subs: Rice (g), Todd

Manchester United: Howard; P. Neville, O'Shea, G. Neville, Fortune; Miller (Fletcher 65), Djemba-Djemba (Silvestre 80); Ronaldo, Scholes, Giggs (Saha 69); Rooney.
Subs: Ricardo (g), Bellion

Referee: P. Dowd

Attendance: 9,033

So, after what Sir Alex Ferguson described as 'the worst performance I have ever seen by my team in the FA Cup', it was off to the park of St James rather than the coast of South Africa, where United had lined up a pleasant mid-season jaunt.

The BBC, naturally, chose the game for live coverage, the national media descended, and 9,033 squeezed into the ground. More administrative nightmares for City's tiny band of

office staff. John Motson was back, for the first time since Newcastle were dispatched 24 years earlier, to commentate live on BBC1, but this time there was no ladder to climb to his commentary position. Indeed, no Cowshed and no Big Bank.

Nor was Ferguson taking any chances second time around: he fielded 11 internationals. The gloves were off for United, with the odd exception of Wayne Rooney, on a mild but windy West Country evening. The front four for United comprised Cristiano Ronaldo, Paul Scholes, Ryan Giggs and Rooney, and it was Scholes who proved the difference. Exeter's dogged midfield simply could not keep tabs on the England international, who made sublime use of the space he created for himself, after nine minutes working a one-two with Ronaldo which the Portuguese winger finished by driving the ball between Paul Jones's legs.

If the result seldom seemed seriously in doubt, City did themselves proud and left some enduring memories: Scott Hiley, seemingly hemmed in by the right touchline, deftly nutmegging Ronaldo to extricate himself from trouble; a clear penalty claim, surely, when Steve Flack's presence prompted Quinton Fortune into a blatant shirt tug; Sean Devine finding the net, but from an offside position. As long as left-back Alex Jeannin continued to whip set-pieces into the United penalty area Exeter had a chance of parity, until finally, just a few minutes from time, Rooney rounded Jones to confirm a 2–0 win.

United went on to reach the final, losing on penalties to Arsenal, but for Exeter the match was about more than the result, more even than the £1 million from the two games. This tie created the memories that would, if properly nurtured, draw the city's youngsters back to the ground in the years ahead, in good times and bad. Even after the indefatigable Dean Moxey had long retired. At long last Exeter had made headlines for the right reasons, and the games against United could be seen as a statement of intent. Exeter weren't back yet, but they were on the way.

Back to the League

Perhaps inevitably, after the attention of the Cup run and the inevitable backlog of fixtures caused by playing United twice, City's season tailed off. They ended the campaign just outside the play-off positions, missing out by a point for the second year running.

Inglethorpe had certainly made his mark, and eventually, at the end of the 2005/06 season, he joined Tottenham Hotspur as director of their youth academy. This time, however, Exeter were well off the play-off pace, finishing 11 points adrift in seventh place. The most significant result of the season had taken place off the field, on 16 December 2005, when after a superhuman effort the club came out of its CVA.

It marked the end of the road for Steve Flack, but Inglethorpe had made some judicious signings who would go on to have a profound influence on City under his successor. Lee Phillips finished the season as top scorer with 16 goals. Jamie Mackie, a young striker signed from MK Dons, never nailed down a first-team place but scored four goals.

Most significantly, during the January transfer window Inglethorpe had managed to persuade a disenchanted Matt Gill that there was a future for a talented midfield player in Devon and to sign a contract until the end of the season.

So, as Inglethorpe headed back to London, Steve Perryman was left with the task of discussing compensation with Spurs . . . and finding a new manager.

If anyone embodies Exeter City and their rehabilitation in the years following relegation to the Conference, it is Dean Moxey. From a gawky YTS boy who was actually to be found operating the away turnstiles on the day City slipped out of the Football League in 2003, to thoroughbred midfielder when City returned five years later, Moxey epitomises Exeter's renaissance.

Of course it helps that he is a local boy, who stood on the Big Bank from the age of 11. And it is hardly a hindrance that he scored what has been described as the most valuable goal in the club's history, and also one of the best, that 45-yard effort he launched past a startled Andy Warrington in the FA Cup against Doncaster. Young Moxey – he was only 18 – took his moment in the spotlight with a succinctness that prompted much hilarity on the *Match of the Day* sofa that night. 'Just went for it. Seen him off his line. Dropped in. Happy as Larry.' He also confessed to being a Manchester United fan, and to hoping to draw them in the third round. Which just proves that you shouldn't always be careful what you wish for.

Moxey was involved in Exeter's darkest day, against Southend, in an entirely unexpected way, collecting money on the gate. 'No one wanted to work for the club so they got all the YTS players to do it,' he said. 'I was on the away end and I just remember all this cash coming through. Then they put the home fans in the away end and moved the Southend fans to the Old Grandstand. I just wanted to get in and watch the game but I had to wait about 25 minutes and when I got there someone had nicked my seat, so I ended up sitting on the floor. It was a horrible day and hard to watch. In one way it was lucky for me, though, because if we had stayed up I'm not sure I would have been kept on.'

With Eamonn Dolan giving youth its chance, it would be a mere five months before Moxey made his debut, in an LDV Vans match against Hereford. Tall, and with a phenomenally athletic if slightly bow-legged physique, Moxey's versatility led to his occupying all the positions down the left-hand side of the pitch, weighing in with numerous important goals, and wearing the captain's armband on occasion.

However, there was a time when he might have left for Cambridge United. 'Football's ruthless and you have to think about number one. Under Alex

Dean Moxey with his FA Cup player of the round award.

Inglethorpe I wasn't playing. They offered me another contract, but I wasn't sure about taking it. It was a hard decision for me but I'm glad I took the right decision and stayed.'

Youthful Promise

Over the years, Exeter have uncovered a number of excellent players, although they have tended to specialise in frail-looking ball-players who appear to be no more than nine stone wringing wet. Martin Ling, Mark Robson and Martin Phillips all spring to mind. All forced their way into the City first team as teenagers, all made mincemeat of some of the less dextrous lower-division defenders, and all eventually played in the First Division/Premier League, Ling with Swindon and Robson at Tottenham. Exeter had particular cause to be grateful to Alan Ball and Manchester City for paying £500,000 for Phillips. Ever the enthusiast, Ball said, when he was City manager, that Phillips could become Britain's first £10 million player; but, frankly, City were grateful for a twentieth of that fee in the teeth of a previous financial crisis in 1995.

The rather more robust Nicky Marker played more top-flight football, for Blackburn Rovers, than any of the aforementioned trio, but for the most famous Exeter old boy of all you have to go back to Cliff Bastin. Born in Heavitree, he played 17 games for City before being snapped up by Arsenal, where in the 1930s he won five First Division titles, the

FA Cup twice, and 21 England caps. A stand at St James Park bears his name, but the search for the next Cliff Bastin goes on.

For Julian Tagg, the youth system is not only the lifeblood of the club but a positive force in its own right. Tagg coached Dean Moxey for three years before Eamonn Dolan, newly appointed as head of youth, took over, when Moxey was 14. 'Everyone had spotted Dean Moxey's potential because he was exceptional,' Tagg said. 'He played a "year young" for the first three or four years.

'The first year we had just a few fixtures, but then, when the club put in for funding for its centre of excellence, we had the nucleus of our first team, in 1998. I still have the reports of how all the players did in each game.

'Eamonn Dolan was the centre of excellence manager, and I became totally involved. He had a work ethic like you've never seen, so keeping up with him was quite a commitment when you have coaching on a Tuesday and Thursday night and both days at the weekend.'

Almost immediately, though, the question of finance reared its ugly head. 'The FA put in £120,000 a year, but the club had to find £40,000,' Tagg explained. 'If you missed a payment you were in double jeopardy because you had to make it up the next year. Because payments weren't being made by the club, we undertook a huge fund-raising task and raised £50,000 to £60,000 a year, which we have been doing ever since. One scheme we did was "Can't afford a racehorse, buy a football team".

'There's a pub in Tiverton, The Barley Mow, that paid £2,000 for a team, and when Jamie Hatch was transferred to Southampton they were given a cheque for £12,000 as their share of the proceeds on the pitch. Others had teams with Deano and George Friend in, and have even opted not to take all the money they were entitled to. The Trust were one of the first to sign up. We did that for six or seven years and got the finances square, and it was at that point that Russell and Lewis took £60,000 from the account.'

When City were relegated from the Football League, the FA's grant was halved. The easiest thing to do, as other clubs have opted to when dropping out of the League, would have been to scrap the youth system entirely. However, with a transfer embargo on new signings, Tagg was adamant it must stay, and the club has reaped the rewards, both on the pitch and financially.

'I have always been committed to ensuring the

George Friend made swift progress to the first team.

finances of the youth stayed separate from the club where possible,' Tagg said, 'but during the last six or seven years the youth has ploughed back into the club £1.2 million from transfers.

'Simon Hayward [the head of youth] has done an exceptional job and doesn't always get the recognition for it. I'm trying to make sure people do know who he is. The facility is at an exceptional level and gives a good deal of opportunity to young players.' The progress of the likes of Liam Sercombe, George Friend and Danny Seaborne stands as testament to that. 'There's a lot of work gone on behind the scenes. We have a team of coaches, including Kwame Ampadu and Shaun Taylor [both former players], but we are going to have to improve because, arguably, would George or Dean have made it if they had been thrown in at somewhere like Leeds United instead of

Droylsden? Their first games were in the Conference, which by definition they are going to be able to handle better than Division One.'

While supporters like nothing better than watching a local boy making good, Tagg said that the strength of the youth system can be felt even closer to home. 'It's about the boys of Exeter having an opportunity. Bearing in mind that 95 per cent won't make it, they will still become positive individuals and they will be fit and disciplined. Most will become supporters of Exeter City and a significant number have become employees, helping to coach the next generation of children.'

One innovation City can be particularly proud of is a retention programme that helps players who have not made the grade. This can have an unexpectedly positive outcome, such as in the case of Elliott Frear, who was released at 14 but later earned himself a professional contract after prospering at the academy the club runs in partnership with Exeter College.

Under the club's Football in the Community programme run by Jamie Vittles, children as young as three years old can play for fun as 'Tiny Tots'. For those select few who are eventually taken on as professionals, the commitment from the club is colossal, and the boys can expect to have had a thorough footballing education alongside academic work. 'Between the ages of nine and 18, Dean and George trained for 800 hours,' Simon Hayward said. 'Now a player will have been with us for 6,000 hours. I will stick my neck out and say that the next crop are better and we can expect two players a year making it into the first team.'

Meanwhile, at Team Bath.....

The American-sounding Team Bath only started in 1999, a novel experiment that aimed to combine the ethos of a full-time football club with the environment of a university. The rationale was that young players who had slipped through the net of the professional game could combine full-time training with a university course.

It proved a remarkably successful experiment, with dozens of former professionals passing through their ranks, graduating from the university and often rejoining the professional game. Team Bath sped through the leagues, winning Western League Division One in 2000 and the Premier Division in 2002. Thus elevated to the Southern League, they moved up again to Conference South in 2008.

The students made national headlines in 2002

Paul Tisdale marks Liverpool's John Barnes while playing for Southampton in 1995.

when, as the first university team to enter the FA Cup since 1881, they made it through four qualifying rounds to the first round proper, before losing to Mansfield Town.

At the helm of the football section of this innovative set-up was Paul Tisdale, who had played 10 games on loan for City in the middle of the 1997/98 season. He was still only 33. Like Eamonn Dolan and Alex Inglethorpe before him, he had played for the club, had been forced to retire early – in his case because of a back injury – and had an excellent record in developing young players. It sounded like a promising CV.

The Interview Process

For a man who has become synonymous with snappy dressing, Paul Tisdale's interview for the job of Exeter City manager was unusual to say the least. For a start, he attended in T-shirt and jeans after the club put back the interview by a day to allow him to return from holiday.

That may not seem like ideal preparation, but Tisdale was in no hurry to leave Bath. 'The flight got back to Bristol at 2 p.m. and the interview was here at 3.30, so I came straight down to Exeter while my wife got a lift back to Bath. I came here with the attitude that I did not want to leave Team Bath. That was my club. That's the type of person I am, so it had to be a damn good reason why I should leave. So I had a good chance to interview the panel: Julian Tagg, Steve Perryman, Denise Watts [chairman] and Rob Doidge [from the Supporters' Trust].

'There was only one player's name I knew – Lee Phillips. I hadn't seen a Conference game but the culture was right and the interview was about development of players, the centre of excellence, so it felt right. I didn't ask about budget, salary or what they thought could be achieved. It wasn't an issue for me; it was whether I fitted with this club. I came to get the job and I thought I'd decide afterwards whether I wanted it. It took me the weekend.'

Tisdale's opponents were formidable: Shaun Taylor was a City legend who had captained the 1990 Championship-winning team, while Jimmy Quinn had led Shrewsbury to promotion from the Conference in 2004. There was little doubt who of the three was lowest on the supporters' radar, but for Perryman, Tisdale's qualities were immediately evident. 'He was very forthright. He was able to convey his message. He said what he thought. He was very clear in his head and that's his great strength.'

Tagg was similarly impressed. 'We didn't know much about him at all, but for me, particularly, what he had done at Team Bath was phenomenal. I'd worked with 16- and 17-year-olds and he had taken the next step up.

'The temptation in football is always to go with the name and the man with the track record. Both Shaun Taylor and Jimmy Quinn were exceptionally good candidates but what the club needed was someone who would understand the whole ethos of what we were trying to do and he obviously grasped that very quickly. I am not saying the others wouldn't have, but it became obvious very quickly that this was an intelligent man and there was a direct affinity.

'It was almost as if he was from a different world. He's an educated man, and the thing I liked was that he was keen not to replicate his own experience in football. The fact that he wanted to do things differently was music to my ears. Conventional wisdom prevents original thinking

Lee Phillips in the wars.

and it was very plain that Paul was definitely not a conventional thinker.

'Steve knew of him and was the one who got him involved, but it was still a big risk because the fans want a name.'

An International CV

Paul Tisdale was born in a military hospital in Malta in January 1973 but remembers nothing of the Mediterranean island as his father, who worked in the Admiralty, brought the family back to England after six months.

As a boy, Tisdale's passions were cricket and football, and they often competed for his attention. He attended the sport-orientated Millfield prep school for two years but decided it was doing his football no good and moved to Beechen Cliff boys' school in Bath.

Tisdale was an opening batsman, and he represented the Somerset Association and Avon Schools until he was 18, and played for the West of England under-15s. He also turned out for England Schoolboys at football and was offered an apprenticeship at 16 by Southampton but turned it down. 'Cricket was probably my best sport, my real passion,' he said. 'Part of the reason I turned down the apprenticeship was education, part that I didn't want to leave home, and a big part of the equation was that I wanted to carry on playing cricket.' So, in the sixth form, he spent three days a week at school studying for A levels in English, Art and Law, and two days at Southampton.

With such a sporting background it was clear in which direction his career would take him: he became an accountant. No, obviously he signed as a professional for Southampton at 18 and spent seven years at The Dell. His appearances in the first team were limited, however, not least because of the consistency of Northern Ireland international Jim Magilton. Tisdale scored one Premier League goal for Southampton, in a 2–1 defeat at Manchester City in March 1996. A report said that he 'took one touch and delicately lifted the ball over goalkeeper Eike Immel'.

He moved to Bristol City in 1997 and, a year after his spell at Exeter, Tisdale found his way, via Scotland and Finland, to Panionios in Greece and a memorable meeting with Sven-Goran Eriksson's Lazio in the quarter-finals of the Cup Winners' Cup in 1999. One of his team-mates in Greece was former Manchester United striker Mark Robins, who has gone down in history as the man credited with 'saving' Alex Ferguson's job by scoring an FA Cup third round winner against Nottingham Forest in 1990. 'As you would imagine, Paul was very professional,' Robins recalled. 'He was a footballer, he was a player, and he worked hard. It is difficult to say what his main attribute was because he was a bit of everything: he closed down, he'd get forward, he'd do a bit of defending. He could get his foot in, but he could pass the ball and keep possession. That was his game and that was how he was brought up at Southampton. You keep the ball, keep it moving, and once you lose it you get your shape and break things up, and that's what he did.'

Robins also said it was clear that Tisdale had a future in coaching and management. 'He was a very, very professional guy but he was a studious type and it was no surprise when he went to Team Bath and did well when he cut his teeth in management there. And obviously when he was appointed manager of Exeter, he's done a great job there. In fact, Paul came right at the end of my time in Greece when I was getting really pissed off. We weren't getting paid and pretty soon I came back to England.'

But not before those two big European nights against Lazio. 'Sven was in charge and they had some top, top players. Fernando Couto and Mijailovic at the back, the Chilean striker Marcelo Salas, and Ivan de la Pena in midfield. They were incredible players and they beat us 4–0 and 3–0, but it was a real good experience.'

Tisdale was soon back in England, too, and aged 26 he joined Team Bath, although while the club was being established, he played 15 times for Yeovil in the Conference. 'I didn't achieve what I wanted to in my playing career,' he said, 'or should have achieved in the 10 years I did play, but I got to the point where I couldn't train daily because of my back. I do have this sense that I want to achieve, and perhaps that is why I am so driven in what I do now.'

Bath Time

Managing Team Bath was unusual in one respect: players left as soon as they had graduated, so only stayed for three years. In other respects, it was like a conventional club side.

'Team Bath was a professional football club design within an academic environment,' said Tisdale, 'like a collegiate set-up, so I was a full-time football coach – I wasn't a lecturer or a PE teacher. For seven years, my job was building a team, which changed every year as students left. I had to get them through the door and work it out. That's how I am now: I have no design on which is the best system to play; you work it out and play to the strengths of the players. That was my apprenticeship. There were 14 head coaches for other sports and you worked together every day. Every Monday you sat and debated with these other elite coaches, like Brian Ashton [the former England rugby coach].'

Bertie Cozic is a French midfielder who came to England to take a Masters degree in sports, found himself playing for Team Bath under Tisdale, and followed him to Exeter. 'I don't see many changes from that time,' said Cozic. 'It doesn't matter for him whether it's a professional club or part-time. We were training twice a day – tactically, technically, and working really hard so our fitness was the same. Paul hasn't changed much, although now obviously he is improving the squad and working behind the scenes to build the club. He looks to surround himself with good people to help him off the pitch, but he is the man, and the way he wants the team to play is the same, whatever the level. From the start at Team Bath he knew what he wanted, in training and on the pitch.'

City Time

Eight years had elapsed since Tisdale's brief spell at Exeter but he found some things pretty much unchanged. 'The Cat & Fiddle training ground still looked similar, although St James Park had improved greatly. The biggest change was the essence of the playing side of the club purely being led by Steve Perryman. I knew that had changed because I had spoken to Steve a couple of times the previous year, socially, and had an impression that it was not like when I was here on loan, which was a very miserable hand-to-mouth time with not much to be optimistic about.'

Tisdale scored one goal in his 10 games with City, but it was not a particularly auspicious time in the club's history. 'That is no criticism of Peter Fox, who was manager at the time. Peter was excellent, but the whole set-up felt as if it was hanging on a little bit, even though I was only here for two months. Now it felt a different, brighter place because the essence had changed. The talk was of winning the right way, and fair play, though not being soft. The need for an element of football to be played, because that's what the supporters wanted to see; giving people a chance. Properness, if you like. It's not just about football, it's about setting a culture.

'Within two or three months of being here I realised Steve was here because of Julian Tagg. I was interested in working with Steve in my first professional job but the starting point was probably Julian.'

Down to Business

Paul Tisdale was appointed on 26 June 2006, days before the players reported for pre-season training. Alex Inglethorpe had done Tisdale a huge favour by signing striker Adam Stansfield and midfielder Matt Gill before he left but there was precious little room for manoeuvre. 'The budget had been spent,' he said, 'although Santos Gaia and Glenn Cronin leaving freed up a little bit of money.'

Any manager will tell you that his ideal is to have two players competing for each position. Exeter were way off being in that position, but in an inspired move Tisdale went after the experienced Rob Edwards, although it so nearly didn't come off. 'We needed a centre-half because we only had Chris Todd, and Dan Seaborne was very young. Patrick Ada was on trial, so I enquired about Rob, but he decided to go elsewhere, to Carlisle, so we had Jon Richardson on trial. He was captain of the

side when I was here on loan and I just thought that was a really safe bet. A real professional, a team player, someone the fans would be happy with.

'I had made up my mind that my first six months had to be really safe, to buy myself some time to work out what this league was about, so I signed him. Then a week later Rob said he'd changed his mind and he would be interested. I was so certain that I wanted Rob that I signed two centre-halves.

'He only arrived 10 days before the season started by which time I already had a system in place, but Rob was such a versatile player that I knew he could fit in. His signing was key because he was the first to buy into really achieving something. He'd left Blackpool, his partner was still up there, and he could have been better paid elsewhere, but I think that he fancied being a part of something different.'

The *Times* business section later became interested in Tisdale's methods, particularly his friendship with Ray Kelvin, the founder of Ted Baker, the fashion retailer, and the way the pair swapped ideas. Their article unearthed a story of how Tisdale communicated his expectations to a new group of players. 'We all need to know how we are being assessed at work, and in football it comes down to performance,' he said, 'so I asked the players how they would like to be judged and they said "a mark out of 10, please". I then thought about it and came up with a theory to explain how I was judging them, so there were no grey areas. It is pretty obvious to me that an employer should be giving the employee the criteria for their performance.

'On a whiteboard, I told them I was looking for at least six out of 10 – that's the line between success and failure. Two out of the 10 marks come from your physical fitness, whether you can play 90 minutes at a time. Another two come from your attitude, and a further two for your tactical understanding. Then there are two more for technical ability, and the last two for star quality. On that basis, you can score six out of 10 without even touching the ball, just on how you apply yourself for the team. You don't start off with star quality, you start with physical ability and take it from there, adding your technique and so on. The star quality comes later.'

Rob Edwards

When Rob Edwards signed for Exeter, aged 33, he appeared to be in the autumn of a long career that

Rob Edwards makes the game look effortless.

big, but the people running the club were far more professional and had been in the game longer. Steve Perryman was here and obviously Paul was just a young manager, but I thought, This place is going to do well for itself. I knew I had a lot of football left in me, it was just a question of starting to love the game again. As soon as I came down and saw how many good young players there were, and what an ambitious manager Paul was, within two or three weeks I was loving it again.'

What Tisdale gained, apart from an innate footballing ability, was a leader on the pitch. 'When I first started playing, Paul Buckle was the assistant manager and he was basically doing the same role I've been doing for the past couple of years. I know what Paul Tisdale is thinking and try to help out the players on the pitch. I remember when Paul drove me down to the Cat & Fiddle on my first day, he said, "What I want is for you to be a bit more concerned for everyone else, rather than yourself. Don't worry if you're not playing well yourself, you've got to try and add value to everyone else by helping them."'

Starting off at centre-half, Edwards's versatility has seen him play left-back, as part of a three-man defence, and as a defensive midfield player, with equal aptitude. It has also helped prolong his career. 'All through my career I've played here and there, and one of Paul's biggest strengths is that he makes sure he has people in their right positions, doing the things they are good at. Paul's helped me by putting me in the right position as I've got older.'

Matt Gill

If Rob Edwards came to Exeter with nothing to prove, the same could not be said of Matt Gill, an obviously talented midfielder who had lost his way in the game, though suggestions that he was about to quit football for life as a tennis coach have been overstated. 'I had put plans in place to take my coaching course that summer, just in case, because my brother is a coach and we own a tennis club together and it seemed a good idea, with dropping out of the league, to have a back-up plan,' Gill explained. But like Edwards, his signing had an element of fortune about it.

'I was a little bit low, having not played for Notts County for a while, when I signed a short-term deal with Exeter at the end of the previous season. We'd seen two or three managers come and go at Notts County. The manager who signed me went very quickly so I was desperate to get out and play

had brought him four caps for Wales and successful spells at Bristol City and Preston. The idea that he would barely miss a match for the next three years seemed improbable, but over that time it is remarkable how many key City moments stemmed from an Edwards pass or free kick.

Yet he came close to jacking it all in. 'I had had a bad couple of years at Blackpool and I wasn't enjoying my football, so if I hadn't found a club like Exeter I would probably have looked to do something else or gone into coaching.'

It was partly a quality-of-life decision. 'Paul and I were friends from when he was at Bristol City for a year, and we stayed in touch. Carlisle offered me a short-term deal and I was going to go for that, but my partner's from Bristol and when we looked into moving back there and playing for Exeter it all fell into place.'

Nor did Exeter seem like quite the step down others might have imagined. 'I would have to say that Exeter were better run than Blackpool. Not as

Matt Gill battles to shake off his marker.

some football. Alex [Inglethorpe] asked me to come back down that summer but my wife had a job in Nottingham and Alex was really helpful in getting us both down, and my wife ended up doing a Masters at the university. I signed, and we went to Portugal on holiday. Then two days later he rang me and said he had left, which was a massive shock. I thought, Here we go again, but fortunately Mr Tisdale liked me.

'He was very different to anything I had been used to. I remember back to that first day: Julian Tagg walked in, then Steve Perryman, then Paul, and he stood behind them for probably the first 30 to 40 minutes of Julian talking, which was a bit different, but we started to get to know what sort of character he was.

'From then on he started to take pre-season training and was quite quiet. He didn't want anyone calling him "gaffer". It wasn't until the Team Bath boys came down a year later that "Tis" caught on. I always called him Paul or gaffer, but if I did he used to make me do 10 press-ups. He got us all together one day and said that if anyone called him gaffer he'd make them do press-ups. The only way we would be allowed to is if we could tell him what it meant. None of us could, but he came up with what it actually says in the dictionary. So, definitely a bit different.'

The Conference is a notoriously difficult division to get out of – in the right direction, at least. As the first victims of two-up-two-down, in 2003, Exeter might have had good reason to curse the doubling of the promotion and relegation between the Football League and the so-called Fifth Division, and, in truth, the professional game had always done everything in its power to keep the amateurs at arm's length.

Until 1987, a quaint system in which the teams at the bottom of Division Four had to apply for re-election was in force. It was a fate which befell Exeter twice, and Hartlepool a record 11 times, but the closed shop meant that most applications to remain in the 92-club League were successful, with only the occasional sacrifice, such as Barrow, Workington or Southport, to allow in new blood – Cambridge United, Wimbledon and Wigan, respectively.

Over the years, however, the League's resistance to change became increasingly anachronistic as the lower orders grew stronger and increasingly professional. So, in 1987 the Football League agreed to one automatic promotion place; then, a mere 16 years later, the Conference secured a second spot, to be filled by the play-off format which had proved so popular, and lucrative, higher up the pyramid. This was still a long way short of the four teams who move from League Two to One each year, but substantially better odds for the protagonists and a welcome infusion of new blood for the Football League.

By 2006, Exeter had tried and failed to make the top five places in the Conference on three occasions, let alone the coveted automatic promotion spot for the champions, and although Paul Tisdale's reign as City manager began with a useful goalless draw at York, it soon became clear that Oxford United would be the team to catch.

Newly relegated, and comfortably the best-supported team in the division, Oxford were led by the vastly experienced Jim Smith, and swept all before them for three months, winning 13 of their opening 18 games and drawing the other five. A certain Steve Basham was a regular scorer, including the winner against City at the Kassam Stadium in September.

However, football is nothing if not unpredictable, and by New Year's Day 2007, when City beat Oxford 2–1 at St James Park, Oxford had lost top

Jon Challinor always had an eye for goal.

spot to John Still's Dagenham and Redbridge (who powered on to win the division by 14 points). City's prospects appeared modest as they hovered in eighth place.

A Pragmatic Approach

As with any new manager, Paul Tisdale wanted time to acclimatise. It's a commodity in short supply at any football club, but Tisdale found he was fortunate to have Steve Perryman alongside. 'Instantly, I was coming into an environment where there was a constant,' he said. 'I wasn't starting

Player and assistant manager Paul Buckle.

with a mess in front of me. It was very well organised in terms of the principles of the way the football side was run.

'As I've got to know Steve more, he has become very important because we see eye to eye on many things and he has been a real aid to my job. I see us as partners, not as director of football and manager, and he has been invaluable because we share the workload and he is good at the one thing I was slow with – the networking and contacts, which, rightly or wrongly, is ingrained in the game. Steve has an immense network of contacts. Most importantly, we speak the same language when it comes to football and we get on very well, so he's very important, not just to me but to the club and the way the process works here.'

As for the players, Tisdale was keen to lay down a few principles. 'The team had to believe in what we were doing. I told every member of the first-team squad that they were all going to get their chance. That wasn't charity, that was a statement that they all had a chance for another contract and to be part of the team. I can remember the crowd bemoaning the fact that I used to rotate Jon

Challinor, Andy Taylor and Dean Moxey every two or three games; Adam Stansfield, Lee Phillips and Jamie Mackie the same. I was true to my word, although I kept the back four the same because that was safe. It was very tight. We didn't open the game up and kept it very pragmatic. None of this football that people have spoken about that the team have played over the past couple of years, but that was my choice, to make sure we didn't make mistakes and to give me some time.

'My aim was to buy myself some time until Christmas to understand the league. By the time of the Burton game [a 1–0 away defeat at the end of November 2006], which was live on Sky, it was clear that we were a good football side but we didn't have that cutting edge and we needed a bit of width. It was then that I went on the hunt for a right- and left-sided player.'

City Sign Rijkaard, Gullit and Van Basten

Wayne Carlisle was a familiar name to Exeter fans: he had played six times the previous season before a broken leg cut short his spell under Alex Inglethorpe. As seemed to be the case so often, there was an element of chance about the former Northern Ireland under-21 international joining City for a second time. 'I was about to sign for Salisbury,' said Carlisle, 'but I was in contact with a few of the lads and they were saying, "We could do with you." I was invited down to play in a friendly against Dawlish. Paul Tisdale played right-back, and he gave me some passes that day, I can tell you! No, to be serious, in everything he does he is tidy and calculated and steady. That's the kind of person he is. But after the game he asked whether I was prepared to do a short-term deal so they could have a look at me.'

At the annual Football Writers tribute dinner in January 2007, the author asked Oxford manager Jim Smith what he thought of Exeter's promotion prospects, and he just drew on his cigar and chuckled. Well, it had been a long and well-lubricated evening and I doubt Jim recalled the exchange as Exeter began to close the gap, but almost at that precise moment Tisdale was moving into the transfer market in a serious way, securing three players from Weymouth: right-back Steve Tully, winger Lee Elam and striker Richard Logan, an England youth international and Ipswich first-team player by the age of 17 whose subsequent career had not reflected his obvious natural ability. The season was about to move up a gear.

'We took advantage of Weymouth's financial situation,' said Tisdale. 'We were looking for players and I felt there was a real chance for a bit of impetus. It could have been two other wide players – it happened to be Wayne and Lee Elam. I took a punt on an additional right-back, in Steve Tully, because I just guessed that Danny Woodards was going to go [he joined Crewe for £30,000 during the January transfer window], so I pre-empted that one, and Logan was the unknown quantity. He could be great, he could be indifferent, we all knew that, but he could be something different and change a game for us.

'I remember being on the training ground the day they arrived and saying that, in the eighties, Milan signed Frank Rijkaard, Ruud Gullit and Marco van Basten and we had just signed the three from Weymouth. It's about buying into something and then fuelling it. Suddenly I had a target man and wingers and there was a pattern to the rest of the season.'

Hat-trick hero Lee Elam (left) and Steve Tully.

Lee Elam's debut could hardly have been more startling: he scored a hat-trick against Weymouth. For the next game he was on the bench and City lost 4–1 at Dagenham, a perennially big and direct team, so when Paul Tisdale attended a fans' forum there was bound to be a lively discussion about his selection policy.

'He had a plan to get a result at Dagenham,' Steve Perryman said. 'It didn't involve wingers, but it did involve bringing them on, and that meant leaving out Lee after he had scored three on his debut. I know how that feels as a manager: you have this feeling to play a particular way against a particular team. It's like with substitutions. When you change a system, the player you take off isn't necessarily the one who is playing the worst. He might be of more use to you in the new system than the lad who is playing better but is the one you do take off. The supporters can't always appreciate that, but Paul is a fantastic communicator: he has won people over with his straightforwardness and his honesty, and the fans and players believe in him. I've never heard him swear. People used to say that he lacked passion on the touchline, but his response to that was, "I find it very hard to think when I'm screaming and shouting."'

Even after beating Oxford and recruiting the Weymouth trio, City's results fluctuated. A particularly punishing schedule of eight matches in March yielded only 10 points, and a 3–2 defeat at Aldershot on 3 April, when goalkeeper Paul Jones was sent off, left them plenty of work to do in the final five matches. However, four wins and a draw secured them the play-off place they had been focusing on since January.

'Beating Oxford on January the first was a big result for us,' Tisdale recalled. 'It was about building a team that believed they were going to win. The imagery was important. It was great when Sky TV started using pictures of Wembley on their adverts for the play-off finals. No one had seen the new Wembley before so, again, it was the players buying into the image of Wembley and believing that we were going to get there in the end.'

He also tried to make the players feel settled. 'People might not know, but the club was renowned for going until the end of the season and having a big clearout and all the players disappearing, but I worked systematically through all the players in December and January and gave them new contracts, so they all knew they were playing for something. They all knew that if they got promoted they would be part of a League Two team and not be abandoned. Even the players [over whom] I had doubts whether they would be good enough to be successful at League Two level if we got promoted, I gave new contracts. That first year was pragmatic, inclusive; imagery, a team going for one target.'

Andy Taylor (right) in hot pursuit of goalscorer Lee Phillips at Oxford.

The Play-offs – At Last

It says something about Exeter's relative lack of success that they had to wait 20 years to be involved in the play-offs whereas certain other teams appeared to have their nerves frayed on an almost annual basis. Terry Cooper's 1990 Fourth Division champions had avoided that particular hurdle by winning the division comfortably, but generally City's players were safely on their holidays by the time the end-of-season nerve shredders came around.

Over the years the format of the play-offs had varied, but the basic two-legged semi-finals with a one-off final to follow was well established. One change, brought in at the behest of Ipswich chairman David Sheepshanks after several disappointments for his club, was the end of the away-goals rule, in which goals scored away from

home counted double in the event of scores being level at the end of the second game. This would prove of some significance to Exeter.

Paul Tisdale's team had finished fifth, only three points behind second-placed Oxford, and therefore hosted the first leg, on Friday 4 May. There was no doubt about the form team, as City had taken 13 points from their final five League games. Even a late Oxford rally, which saw them win three and lose two of their last five, could not disguise a dreadful trailing off in form which could be traced back to the beginning of December.

The tension at the Park was palpable, and it was not a great game. Oxford won it thanks to a bizarre goal when the ball ricocheted around the home penalty area and struck City midfielder Andy Taylor before deflecting past goalkeeper Martin Rice. City's top scorer, Lee Phillips, was absent, injured, and City offered little in attack. At the last, Oxford striker Chris Zebroski missed a great chance to double Oxford's advantage from inside the six-yard box. It was a real let-off for Exeter.

Of his own-goal, the luckless Andy Taylor said, 'It was probably me over-compensating. It came back into our box and then they had a shot at goal. I made my way towards goal to try to stop it but when it hit one of our players on the line it came back and hit me, coming back towards goal, and went in. It was unfortunate but one of those things.'

Tisdale remembers feeling surprisingly upbeat. 'I think we knew we would be better away from home. I found early on that the home games were difficult here. The fans expected a certain type of football and maybe that didn't help us, with players going forward too quickly and being too bullish. I was actually happy we were playing at home first, delighted that Zebroski missed that chance in the last minute. When he did I thought, We've got a chance now.

'We did OK. Oxford left feeling good about themselves and their supporters were celebrating, but we thought, This isn't finished yet. The team were really strong after that defeat. I guess they were relaxed enough to know we'd be so well prepared for that second game and we trained every day. We worked solidly from that next morning.'

And they carried on practising penalties.

Wembley, Here We Come

Oxford United 1 (Odubade 27) **Exeter City 2** (Phillips 39, Stansfield 70)

After extra time. Score at 90 mins 1–2; aggregate 2–2. Exeter win 4–3 on penalties.

Oxford United: Turley; Quinn, Gilchrist, Day; Anaclet (Duffy 60), M. Foster (Pettefer 99), Hargreaves, Rose (Johnson 99), Burgess; Odudabe, Zebroski. Subs: Tardiff (g), Robinson

Exeter City: Rice; Tully, Todd, Edwards, Jones; Carlisle (Stansfield 56), Taylor, Gill, Elam (Logan 60); Challinor, Phillips (Mackie 53). Subs: Richardson, P. Jones (g). Booked: Logan.

Referee: A. Haines

Attendance: 10,961

This was Lee Phillips's most impressive performance in an Exeter shirt. City's vice-captain had a goal disallowed in the early exchanges when he turned in a cross from the left but was erroneously flagged offside. Thanks to TV replays

Adam Stansfield squeezes in Exeter's second goal from the tightest of angles.

and text messages, the City fans at the ground knew almost immediately. City's players didn't, and before they could get a proper foothold on the tie, Oxford's dangerous striker Yemi Odubade muscled his way past Rob Edwards and Chris Todd and hit a shot which, although he scuffed it, had just enough pace on it to beat Martin Rice at his near post.

It took another 12 minutes but there could be no denying City, or Phillips. When Matt Gill struck an enticing flat cross from the right, the muscular number 11 angled an unstoppable header past Billy Turley.

The teams were serving up compelling cup football at its best. The statistics show that Exeter had 14 shots on target to Oxford's seven, and when Phillips's evening was ended by hamstring trouble, Tisdale responded by bringing on no fewer than three attacking substitutes in seven minutes. Jamie Mackie, Adam Stansfield and Richard Logan arrived in a triple change which Steve Perryman referred to as akin to mobilising 'the Red Arrows', although Exeter had a big let-off when Oxford's Rob Duffy froze when clean through and shot straight at Rice.

With so many attacking options at their disposal, Exeter swarmed all over Oxford, and when Edwards struck a diagonal pass from left to right, Stansfield turned his marker this way and that and squeezed a shot across Turley and inside the far post.

City players celebrate as Oxford's Chris Zebroski misses from the spot.

The Penalty Prize

Penalty shoot-outs have destroyed the strongest personalities, but Steve Tully felt remarkably calm for his moment of destiny. 'Tis had everyone taking penalties for six weeks leading up to that game and I scored most times. I'd taken a few for Weymouth so it didn't faze me. We did the whole thing where we had to walk from the halfway line to the penalty spot. He was the referee. It was really professional, and we did it just after training when we were tired.

'At the end of the match he told me I was taking the fourth, but Jamie Mackie really wanted to take one and Tis looked at me and I said, "Well, it's down to him, he's the centre-forward. Go for it. I'll take number six." When Logie had the penalty to win it and missed I thought I had better keep my nerve, but then they missed theirs and I knew I had the chance to win it.

'I didn't really think about the long walk, to tell you the truth. I just kept my head down and enjoyed the atmosphere. I remember looking over to the bench and Paul Tisdale and Paul Buckle both gave me a reassuring look and I just knew, there and then, where I was going to put it. I didn't change my mind. Head down. I didn't even look at the goalie, because that is when you start doubting yourself. I'm very proud and pleased I've done it.'

The away-goals rule would have taken City through at the final whistle, but with the sides locked at 2–2 on aggregate the teams played out another 30 minutes without any more goals. As the prospect of penalties loomed the tension became nigh-on unbearable.

Now, how would City's penalty practice pay off in the shoot-out? Not so well, at least to start with. Oxford went first and scored, but Exeter's regular taker, Billy Jones, hit the post with City's first effort. However, Matt Gill, Andy Taylor and Jamie Mackie all scored before Martin Rice blocked Barry Quinn's effort with his knees.

Three-all, and when Turley, the Oxford goalkeeper, nonchalantly side-footed the home team's fifth penalty against the post, Logan had the chance to settle the contest. He couldn't: Turley plunged to his right to make an excellent save.

Now it was sudden death. Chris Zebroski also hit the post for Oxford, the third successive miss, then defender Steve Tully made the long walk and drove the ball past Turley. Cue delirium among the thousand or so travelling City fans.

City's tactical planning and meticulous preparation had paid off handsomely. 'When you prepare a team,' Tisdale said, 'you have every reason to be confident. It's an anxiety about wanting to do the job, but you aren't nervous about what's coming. We were so well prepared. The subs knew they would be coming on at certain times. In those big games over the past couple of years we had practised so that those people coming off the bench had more information than the team starting, so Logan, Stansfield and Mackie were really well primed as to what their job would be. They knew they were coming on after an hour to go to win the game. The team just knew they were going to win.

'We were practising penalties for one reason only. Not just to be good at penalties but, again, it was imagery. It was Wembley, part of that final six weeks of the season. All about reinforcing the fact that we were going to the final.' Even when they fell behind, not just in the game but in the penalty shoot-out as well? 'No, we just thought we were going to win. We were pretty sure we were going to win.'

> Strange but true. This was Exeter's first victory in a game shown live on television – at the 15th attempt. A succession of cup ties, a local League derby at Torquay and the odd Conference game on Sky had come and gone without City winning, but Lee Phillips and Adam Stansfield changed all that, regardless of the penalties. It was just as well that City ended that particular hoodoo because the following season they were destined to appear on television in live games as never before.

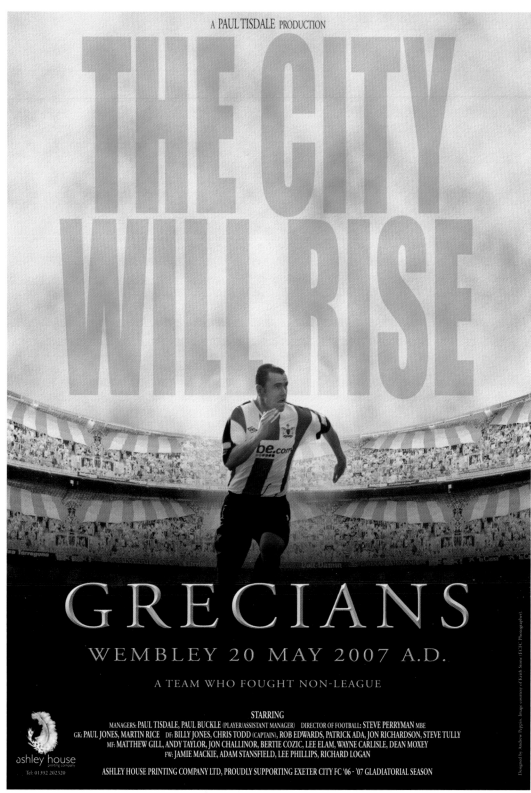

Gladiator Lee Phillips captures the mood.

Exeter players celebrate reaching Wembley for the first time in the club's history.

For Andy Taylor, the result, and his success from the penalty spot in the shoot-out, represented atonement for his inadvertent own-goal in the first leg. 'It was a magical night but a really strange atmosphere. We almost knew what was going to happen that night – that we were going to win. We had a real belief about us before the game and that carried through onto the pitch. Even though they scored first it didn't really deter us from thinking we were going to win that game. It was a fantastic performance from the team and a really enjoyable game to play in.'

The Big Day Out

Nationwide Conference Promotion Final, Wembley Stadium, 20 May 2007

Exeter 1 (Phillips 8) **Morecambe 2** (Thompson 42, Carlton 82)

Exeter: P. Jones; Tully, Todd, Edwards, B. Jones; Carlisle (Logan 53), Taylor, Gill, Elam (Mackie 57); Phillips (Stansfield 36), Challinor.
Subs: Richardson, Buckle. Booked: Todd. Sent off: Gill.

Morecambe: Davies; Yates, Bentley, Blackburn, Adams; Thompson (Brannan 86), Stanley, Sorvel, Twiss (Hunter 72); Curtis, Carlton (McNiven 88). Subs: Neal, Howard. Booked: Carlton.

Referee: M. Oliver

Attendance: 40,043

So this was it – Wembley for the first time in Exeter City's history. An excitement intensified by the fact that the new £757 million stadium had only just opened, more than six years after the legendary Empire Stadium and its Twin Towers had been demolished.

In previous years, Exeter v. Morecambe might have taken place at Stoke's Britannia Stadium or Leicester City's Walkers Stadium. Instead it took place under a new arch, inevitably described as 'iconic', rising 133 metres above the pitch.

Interest in how the Football Association had invested such a vast amount of money on the national stadium was intense. Eight days earlier it had prompted 53,262 to turn up for the FA Trophy Final between Stevenage and Kidderminster. Among the crowd were Exeter's players and staff,

The Paul Tisdale collection, courtesy of Ted Baker.

A brooding sky awaits fans as they gather for Exeter's Wembley debut.

on a fact-finding mission courtesy of sponsors Flybe.

Morecambe had beaten York 2–1 in the semi-finals and were managed by Sammy McIlroy, the former Manchester United midfielder who had also been in charge of Northern Ireland. His Morecambe team were obdurate and physical. Pushovers they would not be.

The City camp was unsettled when goalkeeper Martin Rice responded to being dropped by walking out on the club. Not only did this signal the end of his City career, it meant that Exeter didn't have a substitute goalkeeper on the bench. Ultimately, this proved insignificant because Paul

Jones, Rice's replacement, was Exeter's outstanding performer.

All of this politicking was unknown to the hordes decamping from the trains and buses around Wembley into a party atmosphere. The walk down Wembley Way from the station to the stadium, though only half a mile or so, has always been one of the most atmospheric journeys in football, a heady mixture of nervous anticipation and awe at the scale of the place. To be an Exeter supporter that day was uplifting indeed. Although both teams' colours were red and white it was soon evident that the 30,000 or so Exeter fans outnumbered their Lancashire rivals three to one.

A grandstand view for City fans.

Adding to the slightly surreal feeling of striding towards the ground and the Bobby Moore statue for a City game was the profusion of Paul Tisdale 'cravat masks', provided by the outfitters Ted Baker. Consequently, wherever one looked there were small gaggles of 'Tisdales' having their pictures taken.

Once inside the ground, it was clear that, this early in its new incarnation, Wembley still had one or two teething problems. While Morecambe's modest following were all packed into the lower tier behind one goal, Exeter's greater numbers were on the lower and upper tier, with an entirely unpopulated middle tier in between – a serious atmosphere killer. Morecambe supporters looked out on the massed ranks of Exeter fans, but City fans were confronted mostly by rows of red seats.

Exeter were out of the blocks quickly on the biggest day in the club's history and goalkeeper Paul Jones had little to do in the early stages. The

day before, Chelsea and Manchester United had produced an FA Cup Final of unmitigated tedium, but within eight minutes of this game starting Exeter were ahead, and with a goal of real quality. Rob Edwards's quick free kick released Jon Challinor down the right, but instead of crossing immediately he checked back onto his left foot and picked out Lee Phillips, unmarked at the far post, with the most enticing of crosses. Phillips accepted the invitation and planted his header past Morecambe goalkeeper Scott Davies to give City the lead. Then, just past the half-hour mark, Phillips's suspect hamstring forced him off.

Did Exeter sit back, or were they forced back? Certainly the crowd were muted as the back four appeared indecisive and made a series of errors, the most calamitous being Chris Todd's foul on Danny Carlton, giving Morecambe a penalty. However, the unflappable Paul Jones more than justified his selection and responded with an astounding double save, plunging low to his right

Lee Phillips opens the scoring.

Paul Jones blocks the follow-up after saving Wayne Curtis's penalty.

Paul Jones stands firm.

to stop Wayne Curtis's spot kick and then saving the follow-up with his legs.

A lucky escape, but when, three minutes before half-time, Billy Jones was caught out trying to avoid dealing with Jim Bentley's hopeful pass forward with his weaker right foot, Morecambe's Garry Thompson lifted the ball over Paul Jones and into the goal off the underside of the crossbar.

Paul Tisdale made changes, bringing on Richard Logan and Jamie Mackie. As the game wore on, it appeared to most City fans that Exeter were the team forcing the pace in an attempt to win the game. But, as is so often the case, they were caught out on the counter-attack following a corner of their own. Carlton's goal, with eight minutes remaining, was worthy of winning any game as he outpaced Edwards, cut back past Steve Tully and hammered a 20-yard shot high into Paul Jones's goal.

To cap a wretched afternoon, Matt Gill created an unwelcome piece of history by becoming the first man to be sent off at the new Wembley.

Hard to Stomach

Leading then losing in a Wembley final is the worst possible feeling, but inevitably there were mixed emotions after Exeter's first appearance at the national stadium after such a long wait. 'Wembley was a great event for the club,' said Paul Tisdale. 'It was like a steam train getting there. We started the game so well and we were beaten by a better team, which was a shame. In hindsight, am I glad we lost that game? Yes, because I think we coped better going into League Two a year later. I have no complaints whatsoever, but it was a shock we didn't win. We thought we were going to but Morecambe just passed the ball better. It gave us a great experience for the following year, but for the middle hour of the game they were the better side.'

So when he returned to a sombre dressing room, what did the manager say? A rallying cry for the next season, perhaps? 'Like I do most weeks: "Thank you for your effort." I probably say that after every game, except when they haven't given me the effort. I rarely talk to the players after games. I've been in too many dressing rooms where a manager lets off steam for two minutes and it takes him two weeks to recover it, so I hold my tongue.'

Matt Gill had additional cause to be upset,

although his sending-off in the closing minutes made no difference to the outcome. 'It was frustration boiling over, mainly, because we had worked so hard to get where we were. We had gone on a great run in the second half of the season, done unbelievably to beat Oxford away from home, and I could just see it all slipping away. I suppose the red mist descended.

'It was over a free kick. Craig Stanley went over and, as he did so, he screamed out and made a meal of it. I expressed my opinion, and as he got up I was leaning over him. We hardly made any contact, and he made a lot of it. Obviously that was very, very disappointing, but I have always said that the most disappointing thing about that day was losing. I'd have taken a sending-off if we'd have won.'

Goalkeeper Paul Jones was in the odd position of having been probably the outstanding player on the pitch, yet a loser. 'It was devastating. I would rather not have had a good game and won. I would even have taken letting in four goals and winning 5–4. It was the worst. Yes, I had a good game and made a couple of saves, but there's nothing worse than losing at Wembley.'

Wayne Carlisle, who had struggled to make any impact at all, said, 'In all honesty, and I'm not sure how many people know this, but three players were carrying injuries. Rob Edwards was struggling with his ankle and he might have had an injection in it, Steve Tully was struggling, and I had had a hernia for a few months, and on a different day we wouldn't have played. We went away thinking that on another day we could have done a better job.'

Andy Taylor was similarly disconsolate. 'The feeling after that game was probably the worst since I had to leave Manchester United, really. It

Andy Taylor after the final whistle.

was a real gutting feeling that we had come so close, and put so much into it, and just failed at the last hurdle. If there was anything good to come out of it, it was that we learnt from it and it ended up helping us the next year because we put paid to some of the mistakes we made and made sure we got the job done.'

It was left to Steve Perryman to raise spirits. 'The club is progressing all the time,' he said, 'and I think we can come back stronger.' They proved to be prophetic words.

City lost out to Morecambe at Wembley, but within days an old score was settled at Bristol Crown Court. Four years to the month since their arrest following the club's relegation to the Conference, John Russell and Mike Lewis learned their fates.

The pair, and Russell's wife Gillian, had been arrested by Devon & Cornwall Police on 14 May 2003 but it had taken until April 2007 for them to face trial. The court case laid bare the depth of financial mismanagement at the club, what the officer in charge, Detective Mark Sandford, called the lack of 'the most basic financial records'.

Although the sums owed were eye-watering enough – £450,000 in tax and VAT, £66,066 to Exeter University and more than £13,000 to the police themselves – it was the pair's methods that seemed extraordinary. To save money, they dispensed with the services of NatWest Bank and Securicor, who counted the gate receipts at matches – considerable sums of money – and either took the cash home with them in their cars or left it in the club safe over the weekend to bank later.

Paul Dunkels, prosecuting, said of Russell, 'He was broke. He had no assets, no money and no bank account, and certainly had no money to invest in Exeter City.'

Russell and Lewis were charged with four offences each and at the beginning of their trial they surprisingly pleaded guilty to the charge that they were 'knowingly party to the carrying on of the business of Exeter City with intent to defraud its creditors'. Russell also pleaded guilty to obtaining a pecuniary advantage by deception. Other charges, of conspiracy to defraud, were left on file, but the prosecution accepted not guilty pleas to theft and false accounting from Gillian Russell.

In sentencing Russell, Judge David Ticehurst told him he had betrayed the fans of the club and treated it as his own personal domain. When they were sentenced, six weeks later, John Russell was sent to prison for 21 months and Lewis was given 200 hours' community service.

The frustration for some was that by pleading guilty, a trial many had estimated would take up to nine weeks was over in a matter of days and much of the club's past mismanagement remained unaired. The result represented a victory of sorts, but a hollow one.

Mascot Grecian the Lion with Denise Watts.

Eyewitness

Court reporter Catherine Watson covered the Russell and Lewis case for Exeter's *Express and Echo* newspaper and remembers the accused pair's strange combination of incompetence and blustering humour.

When you interviewed them, Russell was like a blunt 1970s comedian, while vice-chairman Lewis was his quieter straight man. Unforgettable moments included Russell breaking down in tears when I questioned him about the financial management of the Michael Jackson charity fund-raiser. Or the time when furious Grecians fans stormed up behind me on the pitch to scream their hostility at the duo in the directors' box.

I was there to see the show come to an end, in the subdued setting of Bristol Crown Court, with less than a handful of City supporters in the gallery. The pair still had one grand finale, when they suddenly pleaded guilty to some of the charges.

They were always pleasant to me and presented a cosy domestic scene as they chatted to their wives outside the courtroom. But the contrast between their out-of-touch demeanour and the disturbing financial shambles outlined in court was bizarre. They were subdued when they entered their guilty pleas.

Outside, Russell was once again the showman,

insisting to his wife, Gillian, that he wanted to get his feelings off his chest. Pointing to his wife, against whom the prosecution offered no evidence, and Lewis, he told me, 'These two people have been treated very poorly.' He portrayed himself as a saviour turned into a scapegoat.

Lewis, not to be outdone, cheerily handed me a synopsis of his autobiography in the court canteen. I could not believe what I was reading, from a man awaiting sentencing. It referred to his time working with the notorious sportsman O. J. Simpson and Lewis's former role as chief executive of Swansea City where he oversaw 'the birth of Cyril the Swan . . . the most famous footballing mascot of all time!'

Cracks in Russell's outgoing persona were starting to show. He was polite but indignant as he told me how annoyed he was that I had written he showed no remorse after his guilty pleas. But he remained unflustered and nodded when the judge later told him he was going to prison. It was Lewis whose face flushed, even though he avoided jail.

The court heard that the pair had not known each other well when they took over the club. Now they seemed as tight-knit and innocent as comedy acts like the Two Ronnies or Morecambe and Wise. As Lewis told me, 'I'm shell-shocked for John.' In some ways it was touching. But for City fans, the pair's crimes were anything but a laughing matter.

City's commercial director, Paul Morrish.

Jamie Mackie and Matt Gill cheer up one young fan's Christmas.

Denise Watts – A Place in Football History

Denise Watts's story is another of the club's more improbable tales in recent years, but for all the right reasons. When she brought her two small children to St James Park in the mid-1990s the odds on Exeter qualifying for the Champions League were probably better than on her becoming the first woman chairman in the Football League.

'When the boys wanted to go to the football I didn't even know who the local team were. When I investigated it was Exeter City, so I brought these little three- and four-year-olds down to this match and sat over in the family grandstand. The first two or three weeks they enjoyed it and I just carried on doing knitting and texting friends, but I didn't really like it because, historically, my family were all rugby people.

'But suddenly it dawned on me that all these fans were really, really supportive and there was a real camaraderie and family spirit going on and I just fell in love with the fans, which is ironic because I now head up the Supporters' Trust, through which the fans own the club. That's where the love affair began.

'As the years went by there were plenty of ups and downs: we got relegated, I worked as a volunteer, then I became a trustee, and I did a lot of work with the Supporters' Trust, was vice-chair and then eventually chair of the Trust. After we

A Paul Tisdale hat-trick.

paid off the debt and were in zero balance I became chairman of the whole club.

'It's the community, the volunteers who are out there every day and the work parties that really keep me going because there have been some very big ups and very big downs with Exeter City. Fundamentally we need to preserve the fact that the fans are the majority shareholder in this club and that they will have a voice in the club as long as it remains a Supporters' Trust. The message to supporters is that if you want to be part of Exeter City Football Club, you need to join the Trust.'

Watts gave up the chairmanship in 2009 during a major restructuring instigated by City's commercial director, Paul Morrish, to reflect the club's improving financial position but she has always regarded herself as a fan in the boardroom. The Trust has a Board of Society with 18 trustees, and two of them, Watts and Roger Conway, sit on the club board. 'We will always be among the fans, and that can be quite hairy. I've been rugby tackled, abused and written about in the paper, but the voice of the fan is heard because we take it to the Board of Society and then a board meeting. We present it on the agenda to be discussed, so that is fan to board in a few days, and there aren't many clubs that can say that.

'When I took over, the directors used to sit still when we scored a goal, but I am a fan and I'm afraid no one is going to glue me to that seat when we score an important goal.'

Exeter's promotion to the Football League in 2008 gave her a unique place in history. 'How many women can say they've been in the Royal Box at Wembley – twice? It is just phenomenal. When I met Delia Smith she said she had no idea Exeter had a woman chairman. She said, "That's the best-kept secret in football."'

A Club in Transition

Denise Watts's elevation to the chairmanship of the club reflected an ever-evolving structure at St James Park. She replaced David Treharne, who freely admitted to being weighed down by the cares of office. 'When you are running a business, the business comes first, and we were having to go to Trust meetings and say that there were things we couldn't talk about. By the summer of 2004 there was a realisation among the board that what we had put in place wasn't really suitable.

'The year 2005 was financially very difficult. Bits of the club weren't working properly. The bar was an ongoing problem and never profitable. We set about trying to buy a bigger stake in the club and I entered into negotiations with the other big shareholders who, by and large, were totally intransigent. They still thought their shares had a cash value, despite all the evidence to the contrary. I have to say that they were mainly old, bitter men who felt that they had a right, having put in a few thousand each year, to enjoy the privileges that went with being a director of a football club. It was difficult to agree with them on that.'

The Trust's shareholding remains at 63 per cent

John Lee of the East Devon Grecians.

and the identity of many of the 200-plus shareholders, many of whom own only one or two shares, remains a mystery. The share register was confiscated by the police at the time of the arrest of Russell and Lewis, and the copy obtained from Companies House showed that no real attempt had been made to update it since the 1980s.

Inevitably there were tensions within the club, some of them profound. 'We were so busy fire-fighting that we didn't have the organisational structure of any normal business,' Treharne explained. Ian Huxham, a figurehead at the time of the Manchester United games, took the club to an industrial tribunal, claiming breach of contract and unfair dismissal. Huxham also claimed £100,000 compensation but, in February 2007, the panel found in Exeter City's favour and dismissed his claim. 'It was a messy, messy divorce,' Treharne added.

'I was glad to step down in February 2006, soon after Denise Watts and I accepted a certificate on the pitch from Jerry O'Sullivan to confirm that the club had discharged its obligations and the CVA was at an end. That was a very proud moment.'

There is, though, he added, a need for Exeter to continue to become more professional. The volunteer, part-time culture, inspiring though it has been, must change. 'I don't think the organisation we've got at the moment is really fit for a club that is as ambitious as Exeter City has become, and that will change. Personally I was glad of the chance to enjoy the football without the politics of the club, but I am so glad that I did it. It was enjoyable and I think the club will do well, but it

has to reorganise itself again. The trouble with the Trust model is that we are in absolutely unknown territory. No trust in Britain has got as far as we have gone.

'There are checks and balances. The directors have to stand for re-election every three years, so we do have the capacity to hire and fire. Although the Trust is a slow-moving organisation, that can be an advantage. The Trust this year will be putting in £75,000. It's a loan, so if anybody wants to take over Exeter City they would have to find about £1.2 million to buy out what the Trust has put in over the years. This for a club which doesn't own its own ground.

'It sounds corny, but it's been a real privilege to be part of something which, in my heart of hearts, if anyone had asked me in May 2003 what I thought would happen – well, this wouldn't have happened.'

Pay a visit to the Cat & Fiddle training ground and you pass through a gate paid for by the East Devon Grecians. If the players are training, their lunch will be provided by the ladies of the EDG. In fact, there is very little at the Cat & Fiddle that hasn't been donated, installed or painted by the volunteers of the EDG, who have put in hundreds of man and woman hours, none more so than husband and wife John and Di Lee.

The EDG only met for the first time in January 2006, when nine people attended, but they now have more than 230 members and the players are regular visitors to their meetings in Sidmouth. 'Paul Tisdale has been a couple of times, and Steve Perryman,' said chairman Gareth Hughes, 'and at least a dozen players. They are really honest. What really impresses us is we have lads of 19 or 20 who could be stereotypical footballers but they're not – they have all got opinions and funny stories to tell.'

The EDG modelled themselves on their North Devon counterparts and the unofficial tag on their promotional material reflects the ethos of other groups around the country: 'Enjoying and supporting Exeter City. Simply a positive bunch of fans who enjoy and care about our club.'

Flying High

It is a fairly safe bet that Exeter City are the only club ever to have flown to Farsley Celtic for a

Steve Perryman flies the flag with Flybe's Simon Lilley.

Conference match. Farsley may be handily placed for Leeds/Bradford airport but the fact that Exeter could contemplate flying rather than undertake a 12-hour round trip on a coach was down to their sponsors, Flybe, who backed the club almost from the start of the Trust experiment.

It may seem odd that any big company would show an interest in a club that might have been regarded back in 2003 – on a corporate level, at least – as a basket case. However, Flybe's marketing director, Simon Lilley, saw a very positive side to the arrangement. 'We wanted to associate ourselves with something at the heart of the community,' he said, 'something that creates passion, and there is no better platform than a football club, especially when it's the only one in the city. It didn't matter to us whether they were in the Championship or the Conference, although I suppose it didn't do us any harm to look like the good guys – the knights in shining armour when the club was in trouble.

'We have flown Paul Tisdale and Steve Perryman on scouting missions and we "secretly" flew Manny Panther down here before he signed, but we are also involved in getting celebrities from the club to take coaching sessions in schools. I now don't want to be associated with a Premier League club, for all the exposure that brings. I'm interested in something that connects us with the local community.'

Club and sponsor have certainly shared some good times. Flybe named one of their aircraft *Wembley Grecians* to commemorate the play-off victory over Cambridge in 2008. 'I think our sponsorship has gone way beyond a name on a shirt,' said Lilley. 'We were flexible in making payments when the club had cash-flow problems and we would like to think that we have played a small part in the club's success over the last few years. I think it helped the club's credibility to have a national brand on their shirts rather than, say, the local builders' merchant, and obviously it made the players feel good about themselves. They were able to fly to away games and to Wembley which gave them a status a bit above the level they were playing at the time.'

And, of course, it beats 10 hours on a coach to Darlington or Hartlepool.

Supporters Direct

Supporters Direct is an independent body, funded in England by the Football Stadia Improvement Fund, which advises trusts on how to organise and acquire shares in their clubs. Dave Boyle, the managing director, is credited by David Treharne with making four or five trips to Devon in a fortnight in 2003 as the club embarked on its venture into the unknown.

Boyle clearly found the Exeter story inspirational. 'Everyone I met at Exeter who was involved in the Trust was a first-class person who wanted the best for the club,' he said. 'They knew something was up in 2002 and they knew it would end in tears.

'The only reason a trust gets its hands on a club is because it's a complete basket case and no one else wants to touch it. The sooner a club can get past the legacy of debt it inherited, the better, and they do owe a big thank you to Tony Cascarino for drawing them out of the hat in the FA Cup. The Manchester United game gave them the chance to wipe the slate clean, and that's what other trusts haven't been able to do.

'The joy of Exeter's story is that there is no sense that the club has reached its zenith; but no one should be under any illusion that it is easy. Everyone ends up working ridiculously hard, but it is possible to do it.

'If every club was run like Exeter, Exeter wouldn't have to work so hard. It's because other clubs are operating by different rules, and running up debts to buy players they can't afford, that it is so hard. To have 3,000 Trust members is astonishingly good. They have persuaded the people of Exeter that it's vital that they own the club.'

But we are getting ahead of ourselves. In the summer of 2007 there was an awful lot of football to be played before Exeter could be held up as a paragon of the Trust model.

The odds on teams that have lost a play-off final returning the following year are not good. The word 'hangover' is an easy one to reach for, and with good reason.

Paul Tisdale freshened up his squad with experienced goalkeeper Andy Marriott, defender Matt Taylor and winger Neil Saunders from Team Bath, and striker Steve Basham from Oxford. It was quite an overhaul, with Jon Challinor having moved closer to his roots by joining Rushden and Diamonds, goalscoring left-back Billy Jones being sold to Crewe, and a quartet of City stalwarts – Paul Buckle, Chris Todd, Lee Phillips and Martin Rice – decamping to Torquay. After the evolution of the previous season, it was clear there was going to have to be an element of revolution this time.

One player who almost left was Richard Logan as his short-term contract was nearing its end. 'Paul did call me the day after the Morecambe game and said they weren't going to keep me. I was devastated, almost in tears, so I texted him to say I'd do anything, take a pay cut or whatever, and he managed to sort something out. It could have gone the other way, I could have just not texted back and left it like that, but I'd loved my time there.' How different the club's history might have looked if Logan had meekly accepted his fate, or if text messaging had not yet been invented.

Buckle's departure left Tisdale without an assistant, but City started the 2007/08 season strongly, racking up 11 points from the opening five games. Not for the first time in his City career, and in spite of his Wembley heroics, Paul Jones found himself on the bench as Tisdale elected to start the season with Marriott, and with Matt Gill serving a three-match suspension because of his Wembley sending-off, Frankie Artus was borrowed from Bristol City to bolster the midfield. Fortunately, he had an ace up his sleeve in the shape of local boy George Friend to replace Billy Jones at left-back.

If the opening month was satisfactory, September proved a reality check as City were thrashed 4–0 at Kidderminster and won just one of their seven matches that month, although Richard Logan's two goals as a substitute at Oxford to rescue a 2–2 draw in front of the Setanta cameras were a highlight. The fighting spirit was clearly still there, even if defeat at Aldershot at the start of October left City well adrift in 12th place. It was

New signing Steve Basham.

only the second defeat of the season but the team were paying the price for being held to too many draws.

To make matters worse, Buckle had turned Torquay into a goalscoring machine. Although Aldershot was only City's second defeat of the season, it left them 13 points behind the Gulls, where Lee Phillips, Tim Sills and Chris Zebroski were finding the net at a stupendous rate.

One encouraging sign among the summer signings was that Matt Taylor, whom Tisdale had signed for Team Bath one week before he left to join Exeter, quickly proved to be a commanding centre-half with an eye for goal. While playing alongside Rob Edwards undoubtedly helped the defensive side of his game, a burst of five goals in six games represented a phenomenal return. Given that he had appeared on the winning side in an FA Trophy Final as recently as 2003, playing in goal for Burscough, Taylor had quickly laid claim to the title of City's all-time most versatile player and he went on to be voted player of the year.

Time to Rebuild

For Tisdale, it was a case of losses, gains – and

opportunities. 'I was gutted to lose Billy Jones – he was the one I really wanted to keep – but I couldn't stand in his way of going to League One. If you are the type of club that strives to develop players, you can't make it seem attractive to the next person you want to sign if you have just stopped someone moving up the divisions – as long as you get a good price, and the fee was £65,000 for a Conference full-back.

'Paul Buckle was under contract as a player for another year and Julian allowed him to go to Torquay out of respect for Paul, even though we could have asked for a fee. He had worked extremely hard for us but this was his chance of management.

'Paul wanted Phillips and Todd very quickly. We couldn't repeat the last season because we couldn't put the same team out and ask them to do it all over again, so I knew we had to freshen things up and I had to come up with something different. We hadn't put them on the transfer list, but if it suits your purpose . . . I wanted Dan Seaborne to have a chance to play, he had impressed me greatly, even though Toddy had been our captain and was a terrific chap. Paul really wanted Lee, and they paid £17,500 for him, and £7,500 for Toddy. It's not a lot of money but at the time no one was paying transfer fees in the Conference. It made my mind up for me and it gave me the great opportunity to start afresh.

'Matt Taylor was one I had wanted to sign: I thought he would be a bit of a surprise to people. We had lost our left-back so we had a decision about whether to buy a new one or play one of our young ones, which meant George Friend. It also meant mistakes and losing points but knowing that he could be one heck of a player, so we went with that. I think it would be fair to say George cost us a few points early in the season with his positional play, but you just knew what a fantastic player he would be when he found his feet. So the club did what the club does and put its faith in young players, and it worked out very well.' Neil Saunders and Steve Basham, too, were well known to the manager, Saunders from Team Bath and Basham from his time as an apprentice during Tisdale's spell at Southampton.

If early results appeared indifferent, Tisdale remained sanguine, even after being thumped by Kidderminster. 'The first half-hour was the best we had played since I had been at the club. We gave away bad goals but I came away feeling so enthusiastic about what had gone before. I wasn't upset by that.'

Russell Osman stepped in as Paul Tisdale's assistant.

An Unsettling Spell

Behind the scenes, Paul Buckle's departure and Matt Gill's decision to relinquish the captaincy inevitably created a period of uncertainty which, in the case of the assistant manager role, persisted until the end of the season, with former QPR man Joe Gallen (briefly) and then one-time Ipswich and England defender Russell Osman (on a temporary basis) helping out. Both Matt Taylor and Danny Seaborne certainly benefited from Osman's defensive know-how.

'We knew we had good enough players when everyone was fit,' Wayne Carlisle said. 'We felt we had let ourselves down the previous year and we could push on, but it was difficult. Bucks had left and it was unsettling because they were a really good partnership. Paul [Tisdale] did the thinking and Bucks put on the training sessions. The two of them worked particularly well together and he was a big loss. Paul tried to replace him but he was left to do things on his own for quite a while.'

Carlisle and Gill shared a house in Exminster for six months, and the Irishman has his own take on the captaincy issue. 'Gilly has always been a good player, he just needed a kick up the arse. He always had passion, he just didn't have the drive to really push himself. Maybe it gave him the freedom not to have to worry about what everybody else was doing and he could just concentrate on himself.

'It was a difficult time. Bucks had left and a lot of the players had an allegiance to him and were

Jamie Mackie scores the opening goal against Torquay.

still in touch, and we had that slow start, and then there was the Jamie Mackie scenario when he wanted to move on. Gilly was too busy trying to play football and organise the dressing room to play with real freedom, but when he gave up the captaincy he could just concentrate on his football.'

Gill's view was even more succinct. 'I have always been quite an opinionated person, I suppose, and Tis is probably the opposite and will let things work themselves out. We probably weren't right for each other as far as manager and captain go, so I just felt it was best to hand that in. In the end it worked out for the best.'

Jamie Mackie Takes Centre Stage

Jamie Mackie's career statistics at Exeter – 87 appearances, 19 goals – do not begin to tell the story of a player who is something of a blueprint (defender Danny Woodards is another good example) of what a spell in the West Country can do for a young man's career.

It was clear when Mackie arrived from Milton Keynes Dons under Alex Inglethorpe that he had pace to burn and the beating of any Conference full-back who attempted to bar his way. What he lacked was a cutting edge. Banjos and cows' backsides sprang to mind.

Still young and relatively inexperienced, it was no real surprise that when City faced Morecambe on Wembley's wide open spaces, which would have suited his game perfectly, his talents were reserved for the bench. A few months later, however, something remarkable happened: Mackie discovered the path to goal. And how. From all angles and distances the ball whistled into the net, 11 times in 11 games, none better than his opener in the Boxing Day defeat of Torquay when he slalomed his way from the halfway line leaving three defenders gasping for air before smashing the ball into the top corner. After a disappointingly slow start to the season, Mackie was clearly the man to get City up this time.

It couldn't last, though. Bristol City and Plymouth had noticed. The latter made an offer and Mackie handed in a transfer request, just before the home match against Oxford in January 2008. With Steve Perryman handling negotiations, Mackie jumped three divisions to the Championship by moving 45 miles to Home Park in return for £145,000 and the prospect of more to come. To rub salt in the wound, he scored within 11 seconds of making his debut for the Pilgrims, as a substitute, against Barnsley, and found time to score a second later in the game.

Apart from the aggravation of the transfer request, Mackie's transformation said much about Exeter's capacity for bringing on a player and then watching him leave. In other words, a fact of life. 'It was about development and getting a player to a certain point, and until you get to that point you keep working through the process,' Tisdale said. 'He found the understanding of what he needed to do to put his talent into action. There's good and bad in everybody's game but the good parts of his game didn't become effective until he played alongside Steve Basham. Steve made his job easy by doing the jobs he didn't relish and leaving Jamie with one simple thought: to concentrate on attacking the goal in certain areas. Steve was probably the reason why Jamie suddenly "clicked", but Jamie had an enormous work ethic – and not just on the pitch. He trained and trained, shooting, turning. A fantastic athlete – strong, quick over long distances, and a tunnel vision to get better. It was about finding the partner, Steve Basham, to get the best out of him. It wasn't luck that he scored 11 goals in 11 games. He earned it.'

Clipping the Gulls' Wings

Exeter had played only four League games in the best part of two months when Torquay came to call on Boxing Day for what turned out to be one of the division's matches of the season.

It was a beautifully crisp, sunny December morning, the TV cameras were there for Paul Buckle's return to St James Park, and 7,839 turned up for a match drenched with more significance than mere local bragging rights.

If not quite a 'must win' game, City badly needed a statement of intent, and boy did they respond, Jamie Mackie to the fore as they stormed into a 4–1 lead. Dean Moxey and Wayne Carlisle also scored, but both Lee Phillips and Chris Todd responded for Torquay on their returns to the Park and City wobbled enough to end up grateful for the 4–3 victory, if furious with Tim Sills for his theatrical response when Danny Seaborne rather naively squared up to him after an altercation in the penalty area.

Seaborne was sent off and suspended for the return a week later, when Sills scored the only goal. But this was not the last City would see of Sills or Torquay this season.

Danny Seaborne learns a painful lesson.

The Push for Promotion

The return with Torquay on New Year's Day turned out to be Jamie Mackie's last game for the club. Tisdale was philosophical when he left for Plymouth later that month. 'Life goes on and he was determined to go to the Championship. I'm not going to stop a young player going there if they really want to and I have always been a big admirer of Adam Stansfield, so it was a case of, OK Adam, in you go, Oxford at home, two goals, brilliant. What a way to take the shirt back. It made our life quite easy really that Adam was there, and such a fantastic team player. He sat and waited for his chance and took it. And the first goal was set up by Steve Basham.'

Stansfield had started the season alongside Mackie and Richard Logan in a three-man attack, but Mackie's departure led to a remarkable burst of six goals in nine League games for a striker whose value to the team is not always measured by his strike rate. 'We do different running for different positions,' Tisdale explained, 'but we never time or measure them – the days of running around the pitches have gone. In football terms, Adam's not a lightning-quick runner, but what he has is incredible speed endurance. He can produce the same level of speed over and over and over again. Some players might be incredibly quick for three runs but their bodies can't sustain it; Adam can run at what might be 80 per cent of someone else's top speed, but he can do it 60 times in a game. Even if he is absolutely exhausted he has got this incredible resolve to

Jamie Mackie and former City captain Chris Todd.

Adam Stansfield, a constant worry for defenders.

keep doing it. He's our best defender because he is the first one. He starts the defensive process with his ability to run and run, and when he runs in behind the opposition that is part of defending because you are actually changing the flow of the game.'

City kept on racking up points in the early months of 2008 and it soon became clear that another spin on the play-off roulette wheel was theirs for the taking. In the second half of the season an impressive run produced only four defeats, all away from home, from the turn of the year – at Torquay, York, Weymouth and Salisbury.

A crucial victory came on a cold midweek game at the end of January in Cambridge when they clawed back some ground and climbed to sixth with an impressive 1–0 win at the Abbey Stadium, thanks to a towering header from Danny Seaborne. Psychologically important, the game was also a key moment in City's season as Tisdale revealed his eye for the tactical switch by stationing Rob Edwards in front of the back four as a shield for Seaborne and Matt Taylor. The true worth of this move would become clearer the longer the season went on.

Rivalling the Cambridge result for most impressive victory of the run-in was the early April game at Stevenage, one of City's closest rivals. Right from the bitterly cold teatime kick-off Stevenage were thoroughly outplayed and seen off by Steve Basham's neat first-half finish. City's fans responded with raucous chants of '9–0 to the Exeter' – the aggregate score from two League games and an FA Cup win. Meanwhile, Tisdale had

freshened the pack again, with Ryan Harley, a creative midfielder from Weston-super-Mare who had started out at Bristol City and was seemingly equally comfortable on either foot, and Ben Watson, a livewire striker on loan from Grays Athletic.

'The crucial bit was Oxford, Forest Green Rovers and Cambridge [at the end of January],' said Tisdale. 'We had Jamie Mackie leaving, we were dreadful at Rushden in the FA Trophy off the back of that, and the dressing room was "dull" that day, so to jump back with Oxford [2–0], Forest Green [1–1] and Cambridge [1–0] was seven really big points for us. Forest Green was a really hard-fought game. They had a fantastic team at the time. Steve Basham hit the post with five minutes to go with a great piece of skill which really deserved the three points.

'The Cambridge game was huge, a big turning point, and Ryan Harley was starting to press his claim. He had been with us since October and was starting to acclimatise to full-time training again and was ready to come in. I had heard he was doing well with Weston. We were trying to increase our football and he was clearly that, a pure footballer, which was a statement I suppose that we were moving towards a more pure game.

'Cambridge was the first time I played 4-5-1. They were nine points ahead of us so that was a big, big game for us. After that the personality of the team changed, with Ryan coming in and putting Rob permanently into that position in front of the back four. That became our stamp for the rest of the season.'

George Friend heads a goal at Burton Albion.

Talking Tactics

It may well have been the successful gambit of moving Rob Edwards into midfield against Cambridge that cemented Tisdale's reputation for making tactical changes, especially during a game, and this was to become an increasingly prominent feature of Exeter's play. 'I'm always very relaxed to do it,' Tisdale said. 'We don't do it off the cuff in games, we practise it, talk about it, and the players are in tune with it. The players understand how different formations work and I hope I sell it to them in simple terms. I'm also very big on the value of the bench. I spend more time selecting the bench than the eleven, I always have done.'

Mention the expansion to seven substitutes and his face lights up. 'Give me nine! I'd have all 22 players available if I could. It's always the last substitute that is the most difficult selection. I love the substitutes and all the options it gives you. I see it as getting the right people to suit the situation. If you've got the best team in the League, just play 4-4-2 and every player is going to beat their opponent. We don't have that luxury so it's my job to match up strengths against weaknesses in systems. It's a way of beating the opposition and bringing out the strengths in our players. It's not about being over clever, it's about giving our players a simple plan that plays to their strengths.'

In the Frame

At the business end of the season, champions Aldershot were out of sight, with 101 points, but City had closed the gap on Torquay to such an extent that only three points separated the teams after a frantic final day of the regular season, when all possible permutations were possible at one time or another. In the event, Dean Moxey's injury-time equaliser at Burton Albion in a see-saw 4–4 draw left the two Devon teams to battle it out for a place at Wembley.

This was a delicious prospect. It was Tisdale v. Buckle; Todd and Phillips against last year's team-mates; Sills v. Seaborne again. It had all the makings of an epic, and it didn't disappoint.

Wayne Carlisle's brilliant half-volley makes it 1–1 against Torquay.

Play-offs, Second Time Around

Exeter City 1 (Carlisle 76) **Torquay United 2** (Sills 37, Zebroski 90)

Exeter City: Jones; Tully, M. Taylor, Seaborne (Logan 74), Friend; Gill, Edwards, Harley; Carlisle (Elam 88), Stansfield (Watson 78), Moxey. Subs: Marriott (g), Cozic

Torquay: Rayner; Mansell, Todd, Woods, Robertson, Nicholson; Zebroski, Hargreaves, Adams (D'Sane 90); Phillips, Sills. Subs: Rice (g), Bedeau, Stevens

Referee: G. Scott

Attendance: 8,276

It is remarkable how many similarities the two legs of City's play-off against Torquay shared with the previous year's semi-final against Oxford: nerves at home, perfectly valid goals ruled out for offside, tactical nous when the stakes were highest, and stunning attacking football away from home to secure victories. Even Chris Zebroski and Chris Hargreaves had moved to south Devon from Oxford to line up for the opposition again. And with local pride to play for, this time the stakes seemed even higher.

Again City were at home first, and they soon hit their stride, passing the ball slickly around St James Park as Torquay looked content to soak up pressure. So the home crowd were aghast when, excellent goal though it was, Lee Phillips crossed from the right touchline and Sills, pantomime villain for City fans, expertly manoeuvred himself into enough space to send a towering header past Paul Jones. It was a rank injustice, but City's attacking 4-3-3 formation was frustrated as Adam Stansfield fought for space against a mountain range of three Torquay defenders.

Parity appeared to have been restored after an hour when left-back George Friend's deflected cross reached Wayne Carlisle, who powered his header past goalkeeper Simon Rayner. But with shades of Lee Phillips a year earlier at Oxford, the referee's assistant raised his flag for offside and got it spectacularly wrong.

Running repairs to Matt Taylor at St James Park.

Plainmoor penalty! Chris Zebroski fouls Richard Logan.

Emboldened, City kept pushing Torquay back, and, within two minutes of coming on, substitute Richard Logan flicked on Rob Edwards's floated pass and Carlisle, without breaking stride, struck a rising half-volley into the roof of the net with his left foot.

A draw would have been a frustrating result, so it was a calamity when in added time Jones lashed a routine clearance against Zebroski who, unlike a year earlier for Oxford, kept his composure to steer the ball into an unguarded net.

If City were to get to Wembley for the second year running, they were going to have to do it the hard way. However, it was noticeable that during tetchy scenes afterwards – Buckle claimed he had been spat at by a supporter in the tunnel – Exeter's players rallied behind Jones and were adamant they could emulate the previous year's comeback at Oxford when they went to Plainmoor.

Ben Watson keeps his nerve from the spot.

Down But Not Out

Wayne Carlisle had the most to feel aggrieved about after City's 2–1 defeat. He didn't need anyone to tell him he had not been offside. 'I knew there and then that it was a good goal. I got across someone at the back stick – I'd better not mention names because they are my team-mates now – and I knew I had come from behind them.

'The belief was always there. We always believed that over two legs we could beat anyone, that it was in our hands. Tis would figure a team out, and when he had figured them out he would figure out

how to beat them, and we would have a game plan to bring us out on top – although even he would have found it difficult to plan for that game, the way it turned out.

'We had a system that worked for us and we believed that on our day, if we got that system right – whether it was 4-4-2 or 4-3-3 – it would bring us out on top against any team. We believed that, so we didn't change anything. We just kept at it. We still kept the ethics of how we would play it, even if things didn't look good. If you stick at it, good things happen.'

Tisdale was certainly not about to berate the hapless Paul Jones. 'It's like any game of football,

The clincher: Wayne Carlisle scores City's fourth.

there's no point criticising or making a fuss about it. I have to remember that my job is to get the best out of the players for the next game. Nine times out of 10 you don't want to tell someone they have made a mistake, unless it's about being sloppy or trying to do the wrong thing. He made a mistake. My job is not to vilify him, it's to talk about the next game and the fact that we have got a very good chance of beating them. We did it last year, so why couldn't we do it this year?

'We played very well. Wayne scored probably the best goal I have seen us score at Exeter, technically, in my three years. That was special, but that's what Wayne was. We thought we were signing a winger, but he was a goalscorer. Torquay played with five at the back and their two front players wide. I don't know whether you would call it incredibly clever or whether they took a chance, but either way we played some really good football but ended up losing. Their first goal was brilliant. To concede that injury-time goal was a killer, but we thought we were up to this and we could go and beat them there. Again we had time to prepare for it and we had that belief that we would win the game.'

The Twenty-minute Blitz

Torquay 1 (Hill 59) **Exeter City 4** (Harley 70, Watson pen 81, Logan 89, Carlisle 90)

Exeter win 5–3 on aggregate

Torquay: Rayner; Mansell, Todd, Woods (D'Sane 84), Robertson, Nicholson; Adams, Hargreaves, Hill; Zebroski, Sills (Phillips 71). Subs: Rice (g), Hockley, Stevens. Booked: Mansell, Todd.

Exeter (4-3-3): Jones; Tully, Taylor, Seaborne, Friend (Carlisle 61); Gill, Cozic (Harley h/t), Edwards; Stansfield (Watson 61), Logan, Moxey. Subs: Marriott (g), Elam. Booked: Tully, Edwards.

Referee: C. Sarginson

Attendance: 6,015

Joy unconfined. In less than two years, Paul Tisdale and Rob Edwards had become hugely influential figures in the history of Exeter City, but their ability to turn matches with their tactical acumen and assuredness on the pitch reached new heights at Torquay.

City's players may have been confident of overturning the 2–1 deficit from the first leg, but a miserable Bank Holiday Monday, a strong wind and an uneven pitch hardly encouraged fluent play. Just as in the first game, Paul Buckle opted to hold what he had and lined up with a five-man defence. He also left Lee Phillips on the bench. Tisdale responded by including Bertie Cozic for what promised to be an uncompromising opening half and leaving Ryan Harley and Wayne Carlisle among the substitutes.

After a bitty first half of rising tempers and tension, City were undone when Tim Sills and Chris

Zebroski set up Kevin Hill to lash a left-foot shot past Paul Jones. Thirty-one minutes remained, but with two goals needed it looked all up for City's promotion hopes for another year. Yet almost before the cheers had died in Torquay throats, Tisdale had sent on Carlisle and Ben Watson and moved the versatile Matt Taylor forward to assist Richard Logan.

Formations are important, but what unfolded in the final 20 minutes that day is the stuff of dreams. For the 1,000 Exeter fans who were there, there will surely never be such a concentrated period of attacking play to rival it.

The fightback began with a goal that summed up the commitment of the team, and Edwards in particular, to retaining the ball. In a nerveless run that carried him from the right-back position to outside-left, Edwards took 14 touches and played two one-twos, before picking out Harley on the edge of the area. Where many players would have chosen to blast the ball, Harley took a touch and threaded a left-foot shot through a ruck of players and into the bottom right-hand corner of Simon Rayner's goal.

Game on. Suddenly Torquay's defensive set-up did not look so astute as Exeter launched themselves forward in wave after wave of attack. A rash challenge from behind by Zebroski on Logan gave City a penalty and a chance to get right back into the tie, and to the surprise of many fans behind the goal it was Watson who stepped forward. He sidefooted a nerveless effort to level the score at 3–3 on aggregate.

Extra time beckoned, but City were irresistible. Carlisle checked back on to his left foot and his inswinging cross drew the deftest of flicks from Logan. Torquay were spent, but City were in no mood to take their foot off their throats, and when Edwards intercepted yet again, Watson chased, retrieved and set up Carlisle for a fourth.

The Warm Glow of a Derby Victory

Tisdale said he had thought long and hard about Ryan Harley. 'Again, I picked the bench before I picked the eleven, almost. I had a clear image of the bench. I spoke to Ryan, who wasn't very happy he wasn't playing, and I said, "Look, you are going to come on and win us the game, please, that's your job today." Wayne was the same. And Ben Watson. I think Wayne probably believed it a bit more than the others because he had been here the previous year. Bertie was in the side to make a statement that we weren't going to get roughed up. I know people don't like playing against Bertie, and I wouldn't, but they had roughed us up a bit there on New Year's Day. We had worked on Matt Taylor going up front as well, to fight fire with fire if we needed to, and primed the subs to come on and believe that they were going to go and save the world. That's the way they have to feel. Even when they scored their goal I still thought we were going to do it. If I don't believe it, why should the players, and then what chance would we have?'

Even the manager could not have anticipated such a goal, though. 'That was Rob's extraordinary moment. Ryan was composed enough to take a touch back and kept it low on his weaker foot. It was a fantastic goal.

'When a team plays against you to defend and hang on, the psychology of the game is hugely different. In many ways, them scoring that late goal at St James Park did us a favour because it possibly encouraged them into being a bit more defensive and hanging on to what they had as opposed to playing their normal game. We had to chase. And when the difference is two goals it is a very strange scoreline. The number of times one goal becomes two. Ryan got the goal, and then the penalty, and Ben picked the ball up. You have to go with the flow and with whoever picks it up. As soon as he scored I knew we were going to win.'

Carlisle's supreme faith in his manager was well rewarded, but after his bravura performance in the first leg, when did he know he wasn't playing? 'As soon as I walked into the dressing room. He hadn't named the team but he made a beeline for me, got in front of me and said, "You'll be doing it from the bench today." Surprisingly, this was not the body blow one may think. 'People always say that it must have been gutting, but I trust the man. I trust him. I had a belief in him and what he was doing. I knew he had a plan and I was involved in it and I thought, Go with it and see what his plan is. And it was spectacular, almost bizarre. I know how it must have felt from their end because I signed for them three months later. It hit them hard.'

If so, Paul Buckle hid it remarkably well. Emerging from the tunnel a long while after the final whistle, the Torquay manager told the local press, 'Don't look so upset – that's my job,' before graciously wishing Exeter well at Wembley.

City were indeed going back to Wembley. This time there could be no slip-ups.

Men with a mission for City's Wembley sequel.

The teams line up at Wembley.

Wembley, the Second Time Around

**Blue Square Premier Promotion Final,
Wembley Stadium, 18 May 2008**

Cambridge United 0 Exeter City 1 (Edwards 22)

Cambridge United: Potter; Gleeson (Fortune-West 75), Albrighton, Peters, Hatswell; Brown (Reed 66), Wolleaston, Carden, Pitt; Boylan (Viera 69), McEvilly. Subs: Morrison, Beesley. Booked: Gleeson.

Exeter (4-3-3): Jones; Tully, Seaborne, Taylor, Friend; Gill, Harley, Edwards; Moxey, Stansfield (Watson 84), Logan. Subs: Marriott (g), Carlisle, Elam, Cozic.

Referee: C. Pawson

Attendance: 42,511

If it is possible to draw a distinction between Exeter's first and second visits to Wembley it would be that the second was more businesslike. The fairydust that had surrounded the inaugural trip had disappeared the moment the final whistle sounded on the Morecambe defeat. A repeat was unthinkable.

This time there would be no trip to the FA Trophy

Final to acclimatise, just a searing realisation that defeat would negate all the efforts of the previous nine months, and in particular the heroics at Torquay.

Paul Tisdale spoke of exorcising the ghosts of 2007, and what better opportunity than a match against Jimmy Quinn's Cambridge, a decent footballing team with the meanest defence in the Blue Square Premier, but one Exeter had drawn with and beaten during the regular season. The same Jimmy Quinn whom Tisdale had beaten to the City job two years earlier.

There were many differences from the year before, of course. This time George Friend would be patrolling the left-hand side, with Dean Moxey, who missed out against Morecambe through injury, ahead of him. Danny Seaborne would be an improbably young captain, at 21, in a very youthful back four, albeit with the insurance of Rob Edwards anchoring the midfield alongside Matt Gill. Up front, Tisdale began with the attack-minded pairing of Adam Stansfield and Richard Logan.

This time, the fan split was almost exactly 50:50 and Wembley had wisely sorted out the problematic middle-tier ticket holders so that both

Rob Edwards heads the winner.

teams' supporters occupied half the stadium, with the upper tier empty. The noise was fantastic, although muted on the City side by fear of a repeat of the previous year's failure.

If the players were entertaining similar feelings, it was not obvious as they slickly played the ball around the Wembley turf. The triangles down the left involving Friend, Ryan Harley and Moxey were particularly pleasing on the eye. Moxey exerted real menace when he trotted over to the right wing to curl in set-pieces.

He had already had one sighter, culminating in Logan heading narrowly wide, when his corner was flicked on by Matt Taylor, and Rob Edwards, gambling on the ball's destination and losing his marker, Lee McEvilly, in the process, powered a glorious header past Danny Potter and through the legs of Courtney Pitt, the Cambridge defender covering the post. On the touchline, Tisdale pumped his right fist while Edwards carried on running towards the Exeter fans congregated behind the goal until those with younger legs caught and submerged him.

If there were thoughts of the previous year, when Lee Phillips's early goal did not lead to victory,

there were no obvious signs of them. City's midfield continued to dictate the pace of play. Inevitably, though, Cambridge began to chase the game, and Pitt's elusive running down the left created openings. From one of his crosses, defender Mark Peters looped a header onto the top of the City crossbar in first-half added time.

Early in the second half, Moxey was incorrectly flagged offside, from Logan's superb diagonal pass, long before he slid the ball past Potter with his right foot and into the net.

It was a tight game, and Cambridge's reputation as a strong team from set-pieces was borne out when Jones failed to make strong contact from a free kick and Matt Taylor prodded away a goal-bound effort by Cambridge defender Peters. There were few moments of genuine alarm, though, and a sure sign of Exeter's command of the game was that Tisdale restricted himself to just one substitution.

The nagging doubt that some beartrap might be just around the corner haunted every Exeter fan, but on the pitch the players made a convincing job of going in search of a clinching second. Moxey's unflagging energy sent him haring clear down the

Rob Edwards's moment of triumph.

left in the final minute of normal time from substitute Ben Watson's neat touch. A square pass from Moxey might have teed up Watson, who was galloping up in support, but he elected to shoot and Potter saved with his legs.

There were three and a half minutes of added time to negotiate, but no matter. The final whistle soon sounded. Relief all round. It was left to Danny Seaborne – young, a local lad and tough as teak – to lead the climb up the 107 steps to collect the precious trophy that brought with it a ticket back to the Football League and a first promotion in 18 years. No wonder the celebrations that followed on the pitch were so exuberant.

A Fitting Finale

Could there have been a more appropriate, if unlikely, goalscorer than Rob Edwards? City's matchwinner was the only player to have started every game during the season yet it was only his second goal, and his third in all for the club.

Yet Edwards's first thought was with Cambridge. 'Morecambe was such a huge disappointment for us. I was obviously delighted for ourselves and I wanted it more than anything, but I know how it feels to lose on the big occasion. I don't know why that was in my thoughts but I did feel sympathy for those lads. After the final whistle I just knew what they would be going through.'

So how had Edwards come to be the man on the end of Dean Moxey's corner? As is so often the case, it might very well not have happened. 'George Friend had been going up for corners,' Edwards explained, 'but a couple of days before the match, for whatever reason, I ended up going up when we were practising set-pieces. I remember the day before the game, a ball came flying in, just like it did in the game, and somebody headed the ball and it went across where I should have run. I thought to myself, If I had run in there it would have been a goal. I remember Steve Perryman on the side saying, "You've got to run at the far stick. Don't look at the ball, just make sure you run at the far stick." So when we got the corner, I ran at the far stick and I ended up heading the ball in the net.'

Adam Stansfield, who ran himself to a standstill in the cause, was understandably elated. 'I could not have imagined doing this when I was back

Matt Gill gets a foot in.

Matt Taylor in commanding form.

Done it! Jimmy Quinn and Paul Tisdale.

The glittering prize.

Unalloyed joy for the Exeter squad.

playing for Cullompton and Elmore and working at Lloyd Maunder, packing chicken. We passed the ball so well, and it is horrible if you are on the end of that and you are constantly chasing the ball.

'It has been so relaxed this year. We ditched the suits and came in shorts and T-shirts and the low-key approach worked. We were so relaxed on the ball. You see Premiership teams come to Wembley and not pass the ball as we did.'

Team spirit had played a crucial part. Wayne Carlisle, who sat out the game on the bench, said, 'Of course it was disappointing not to get on, but again, I believed in the manager. I thought I would get on and he had a plan that was going to win the game and I was part of it and I trusted him.' As it turned out, Carlisle had played his last game for the club.

Fear of failure for a second time was definitely a factor, said Tisdale. 'We didn't expect to win. It was subdued, very nervous. The first time we hadn't contemplated we could lose; this time we knew what it felt like. The first year it was like a carnival at both ends of the pitch; the second year it was

Cheggers on the other side of the camera for once.

Rebecca Lowe soldiers on as Steve Tully (centre) turns the air blue.

just the games he has played, it's his help in creating the environment of the place. He has contributed to the way the culture of the club has evolved, so for him to score the goal was brilliant.'

The Year of Setanta

It was just as well that Exeter had broken their duck by beating Oxford in a live televised match the previous May because in August 2007 Setanta, a fledgling Irish TV station, began a mammoth broadcasting operation that would see them televise 69 games in the newly retitled Blue Square Premier.

This was the year of City on the telly: the promotion final was their 11th appearance in all – almost as many in one season as in their entire history to date. Fans swiftly became used to touchline reporter Rebecca Lowe's blonde head popping up and interviewing all and sundry, and former England defender Paul Parker's over-the-top tackles on the English language, which prompted the chant, to the tune of 'Volare', 'He works for Setanta, he don't know much grammar, Paul Parker, whoaooo!'

Eyewitness

Rebecca Lowe has many fond memories of the 2007/08 season as it represented a big break in her career. It began with battles with Paul Tisdale as Setanta tried and failed to get permission to put a camera inside the City dressing room, and included an infamous interview after the Torquay semi-final when Steve Tully turned the air blue.

> *I covered 66 out of the 69 games. It was an unprecedented amount of coverage, and if you were involved, you lived and breathed it. Spending Christmas night in a hotel in Exeter, before the Torquay game, for instance.*
>
> *There were a lot of innovations, but Paul Tisdale was one of only two managers who refused to have a camera inside the dressing room. Paul's a man of principle and he said no and stuck to it. I think he just felt it wasn't right, which is fair enough, but I thought it was a shame he wouldn't do interviews during the game because he is so articulate and interesting, unlike some other managers. I am sure he would have come out with a few gems.*
>
> *Steve Tully first came to my notice at the Northwich game. I was standing by the tunnel, writing on my clipboard, when the players ran out to warm up and somebody pinched my backside.*

a carnival at the Cambridge end and our end was just subdued. The players were terrified of losing, but we still played brilliantly.'

Exeter's comfort in possession impressed neutrals. 'That was the experience of the previous year,' said Tisdale. 'We worked on keeping the ball because we knew we were better at it than they were. It's a massive pitch, feels big, and we knew how to keep the ball and let the game come to us because we had the team to do it. It was a brilliant team. Moxey and Friend on the left-hand side is a brilliant combination – in fact that whole left side of the pitch, with Seaborne, Edwards, Harley, Friend and Moxey.

'We knew we would win if we dealt with set-pieces, and once we went a goal up, Jones, Taylor and Seaborne were immense – that triangle in front of our goal – and Friend and Tully with their athleticism to block crosses. Once we got a goal up it had 1–0 written all over it.'

And the goal itself? 'We worked on the set-piece. Right place at the right time. Is it chance, is it good play, is it tactical genius? It's a bit of everything, but I'm delighted Rob got it, and I've got the picture of it above my desk at the training ground. He deserved that goal. He's always had injuries throughout his career but in three years he only missed about four games. He's been the main man really for three years, along with Gill and Stansfield, but Rob has been the player because he has reflected the culture of the place. It's not

Players are cheeky, of course they are – I'm a girl in the vicinity and they're not used to it – but no one else has ever taken it upon themselves to pinch my bum! I turned round and it was Steve Tully, and he winked at me and laughed. I thought, He may look innocent but he's trouble.

Six months later and with 20 minutes to go at Plainmoor I was getting ready to interview Torquay's players, but after that amazing turnaround I found myself interviewing Steve, Ryan Harley and Richard Logan. It was quite noisy and you can't always hear what's said, but you have a radar for swear words on live TV. I heard him in my ear and at the same time the producer was shouting 'Apologise, apologise!' so I did and said, 'Steve, behave yourself,' and he nodded and laughed. I went to Richard Logan, and I never thought in a million years he'd say it again, but when I went back to Steve, he did say it again. I don't even think, genuinely, he meant to, but I thought I would get into trouble for going to him a second time. To be fair, he came up afterwards and apologised. The problem was that it was a Bank Holiday Monday in the middle of the afternoon – not a good time to be using the 'F' word on live television.

The final was brilliant. The best programme Setanta did. We did a meet-the-teams with Exeter. It was a beautiful day, not a lot of chances, but Exeter were certainly deserving winners. I'd been at a game early in the season when there were chants from the Exeter fans for Paul Tisdale to be sacked, but that's football, isn't it?

Rob Edwards and Matt Gill were both excellent interviewees, and then we got into the dressing room – finally. I got covered in champagne and of course Paul Tisdale said, 'Come in, it's not a problem.' He always kept himself measured. The one time I really saw him show emotion was after the third goal at Torquay.

What struck me that day was that it might have been St James Park, because it was so normal. They did nothing different. It was business as usual, get the job done and breathe a sigh of relief afterwards. That's Paul Tisdale to a tee.

The Last Word

Every Exeter fan at Wembley had his or her own reason to celebrate, but no one felt the joy of promotion more strongly than Julie Le Milliere, who had married on the pitch on the day five years earlier when City were relegated and whose husband, Neil, runs the London-based Exeter Exiles and seems to like nothing better than organising trips for dozens of supporters to all corners of the country. And some of them have been very obscure indeed.

'The first year everybody enjoyed the Conference and the fan base didn't drop,' Julie said, 'but the novelty soon wore off. I think Margate away, at Dover's ground, was the time when we really knew that, yes, we were a Conference team.

'Wembley in 2007 was a horrible day – we just didn't do ourselves justice. In 2008, against Cambridge, I wasn't the least bit nervous. It just felt right. And, yes, it did feel personal. All I'd ever felt since we got relegated was that I just wanted to get back in the League. That's all I wanted. Everything since has been a bonus.'

Your club has been out of the Football League for five years and won back its coveted status with a famous victory at Wembley. Where else would you choose to begin the season than at home? The doom surrounding the Southend game in 2003 could hardly have felt further away when Exeter returned to Football League action, and, frankly, after five years of travelling to tiny specks on the football map such as Droylsden and Farsley Celtic, even a game against Rochdale would have held a certain cachet. The fixture computer, however, seemed determined not to play along. City would reacquaint themselves with League Two with a 700-mile round trip to Darlington. The longest trip of the season.

If it was possible to draw any conclusions for the 45 games that would follow the 1–1 draw in the north-east, then it seemed the City team would have a settled look about it, that they would score goals from all positions, that penalties would play a prominent part, and that Paul Tisdale's team would enjoy awesome travelling support. Six hundred and four fans made it to Darlington and saw Exeter concede an early penalty following a rash challenge by George Friend in a poor first-half performance. Things looked up in the second half, however, and normal service was swiftly resumed when Rob Edwards planted a free kick on the head of Danny Seaborne and the captain headed the equaliser.

Eyewitness

It sounded like a good idea at the time, but when Exeter supporter Pete Bishop pledged to cycle to City's first game back in the Football League, he reckoned without the fixture computer.

At Wembley, once the noise levels had dropped enough for my friends to hear me, I said, 'Right, I'm going to cycle to City's first away game back in the Football League, I don't care where it is.' I cared a little more when it was Darlington, and my first reaction was 'Well I'm not going there!' But a promise is a promise, so 3 p.m. on Wednesday 6 August saw me set off from St James Park on my trusty 20-year-old racing bike.

The first leg, 95 miles to Bristol, took me along the same roads I had travelled in aid of Red or Dead to Forest Green five years earlier. What a contrast: back then we were doing what we could

Goalscorer Danny Seaborne shows his power in the air at Darlington.

to ensure the very survival of our club. This trip was one of celebration, and in aid of Exeter Mencap. Ahead of me, however, lay approximately 400 miles of road. Eek.

I'd prepared myself a little: for the previous month I'd laid off the beer, and cycled 40 miles each Sunday. Rolling across the Somerset levels was a joy, one of my favourite parts of the world. At 9 p.m. I was in Bristol, and after a bath and cup of tea it was off to a local pub, where I had my first pint for a month.

Cyclist Pete Bishop.

Marcus Stewart working hard for the team by tackling back against Grimsby.

After loosening up the next morning on some of Bristol's hills, it was up the A38 to Tewkesbury, then the Fosse Way to Leicester for the night. On the third day the weather changed and I reached Newark-on-Trent chilled to the bone by the incessant rain. Newark train station appeared but I resisted temptation. After haddock and chips to refuel in Worksop, it was on to Leeds.

The final morning was a breeze – a very strong one from the south, blowing me (and heavy rain) the 70 miles or so to Darlington. I arrived early for the game, so nipped into town and found a charity shop. Fifteen minutes and £11 later I emerged snug and warm in a complete new outfit. It was great to be at City's first game back in the League, where we belong, even after 415 miles in 70 hours.

Oh, and in case you are wondering, I caught the supporters' bus home.

The Grecians made a more awkward start at home, losing their first two League games and two cup ties, but it was soon apparent they had nothing to fear in the division, even given the insurance policy of three teams starting with hefty points deductions for an assortment of misdemeanours: Luton (minus 30), Bournemouth and Rotherham (both minus 17).

A 1–0 win at Bournemouth before the end of August, thanks to another excellent strike by Ryan Harley with his 'wrong' left foot, was a better template for what was to come, and supporters began to look up the table rather than down it, many believing that Exeter would be good for a top-seven finish and another tilt at the play-offs.

Already many of the themes of an exciting season were evident.

Changing Faces

During the summer, three stalwarts of previous campaigns had left Exeter: Andy Taylor, Wayne Carlisle and Lee Elam. John Yems, a man with extensive contacts in the south-east of England, was the new assistant manager, but of Paul Tisdale's summer signings only Marcus Stewart, a prolific goalscorer for Bristol Rovers, Huddersfield, Ipswich and Sunderland, among others, and three times transferred for more than £1 million, started at Darlington. Stewart had been such a successful goalscorer that he was nearing 200 career League goals and 250 all told, but was destined to play a more withdrawn role for City. Craig McAllister, a formidable-looking striker from Grays Athletic with more than a touch of Australian forward Mark Viduka about him, both in looks and style of play, and the magnificently named Emmanuel 'Manny' Panther, a combative midfielder from York City, made it on to the bench.

This was a deliberate policy on Tisdale's part. 'It was right and proper, and actually if Dean Moxey had been fit for the start of the season, Marcus wouldn't have started. Those players had fought hard to get promotion and earned their place in the Football League and were fully entitled, I thought, to start the next season and earn the right to play in the next league first. Marcus was the exception because when Dean came back, George Friend was sold, and Marcus bridged that gap really well; but the others had earned their chance.

'Marcus was a very big signing for us. Most

people assumed we were signing a former striker who had scored his goals at Premiership level, but we were signing an individual who added balance to the squad – and don't forget we are a club that prides itself on developing and improving young players, but you can't have progression and development if you've got a team of younger players who are inexperienced and losing every week. You need that balance and that core structure for them to play off, and Marcus would be one of those who can help them.'

Tisdale spent no money in the transfer market during the summer but he did receive £350,000 from Wolverhampton Wanderers for George Friend as the 31 August deadline approached. It is surprising, given the dearth of left-sided talent in England, that Exeter had produced two of such quality who were born within a few miles of each other, in Friend (from Barnstaple) and Moxey (from Pinhoe). The club accepted Wolves' offer knowing that Friend would have the chance to test himself with a top Championship team and that they had adequate cover in the shape of Moxey. Tisdale never did quite get round to spending any of the proceeds, though.

Manny Panther in full flow.

Tisdale on Recruitment

'By definition you have more players to choose from the higher you go up. There were players who wouldn't have considered playing in the Conference that we can attract in League Two or One,' he said in 2009. 'But the job is no easier or harder because at every step your ambition is to sign players who are capable of being successful at the level you are at, and the players we need are able to earn more money at other clubs.

'Whereas in the Conference we would consider ourselves a top third club, for all sorts of reasons, most of which are obvious, in [League] Two we would probably be regarded as a middle third club and in [League] One as a lower third club. That's not about the spirit of the club or all the things that are great about Exeter, it's pure maths and dynamics really. We are still trying to recruit players to make us a top third club but it becomes more and more difficult, and we are more choosy, so our profile is changing rapidly.

'Geography is still the biggest obstacle. You invariably don't give more than a two-year contract because the club is not able to forecast its figures that well and it is hard for a manager to plan any further ahead. So offering a year or two for someone to uproot and maybe move their family is

not very appealing, but on the other hand this is a big club in the south-west. It's hard to get players down here but once they are here they like it and they want to stay. That's the pull of the area, the fabulous club that we've got and the environment we work in.'

To ensure that a new signing will fit in, Tisdale runs his 'Carlisle test'. That's Carlisle in Cumbria, not Wayne Carlisle, and it's important given that in 2008/09 Exeter had to travel 10,600 miles to and from their matches in League Two. If you ignore the odd flight and assume a generous average speed of 50mph, that means almost nine days and nights together on a bus over the course of a season. 'You have to pass the Carlisle test,' the manager insisted. 'You don't have to be best friends with everyone but everyone has to be sufferable! That is a joke, but when you've got to sit alongside somebody for 12 hours every other week it's important that there is a camaraderie about the place and you can put up with good times and bad times together. It's about being a team and showing that there is more to it than three o'clock on a Saturday. We have a lot of long trips together, and when you build a team it's about relationships.'

Paul Jones: City's No 1.

Top scorer Adam Stansfield celebrates another goal against Gillingham.

Exeter's No. 1

The step up to League Two coincided with Paul Jones finally making the goalkeeper's position his own. Indeed, he was the only ever-present. It had been an interesting journey since that nerveless performance at Manchester United when he was on work experience from Leyton Orient, who were still paying him. 'To be honest,' he said, 'because I was so young and so new to the game it never sunk in about the occasion. I was a fearless 18-year-old who just wanted to do his best on the football pitch. I had no real awareness about the size of the crowd or who we were playing, which seems amazing because it's the biggest ground in England.'

Even by then he had forged a reputation with penalties, having saved one with his first touch in a City shirt, at Dagenham, a few weeks before the Old Trafford game. 'I thought I was going to help with the warm-up so when the manager said I was on the bench it was the last thing I expected. Then, halfway through the second half, the goalkeeper got sent off and I was on the pitch, facing a penalty. Not being big-headed, but I had quite a good record of saving them for the Orient youth team, so I was pretty confident and I went the right way and saved it. I don't have any special technique, I just try to read the centre-forward, and it isn't often I go the wrong way.'

Jones had to endure long spells out of the team, however, understudying Martin Rice and Andy Marriott. 'When Tis came in I didn't have a good pre-season and didn't start the season, and that was quite frustrating. Luckily I have a very good

goalkeeping coach in Mel Gwinnett and he had a quiet word with me, settled me down and got me focused on what I had to do and what I could achieve. I have always listened to him and he has always pushed me, and I hope I am reaping the rewards for that.'

Born in Maidstone, Jones still has a Chelsea season ticket in 2009, though he seldom gets to use it. 'I went to every game from the age of 11. I haven't been for ages, but my dad's not going to give it up, in case he loses it.' Although he still thinks of the south-east as home, Jones is almost part of the furniture. 'I won't say I feel old but I'm not far off 200 games and I've just turned 23. I'm the longest-serving player, which is quite strange.'

Continuity

The fact that Exeter's starting line-up had a settled look for the first two months of the season was frustrating for Manny Panther and Craig McAllister. Panther went to Rushden for some match practice and managed to get himself sent off twice, McAllister was shown a red card in a reserve game against Plymouth. Both would more than play their part as the season unfolded, but in the meantime City were scoring goals from all over the pitch. Indeed, they failed to score on only four occasions before Christmas.

Adam Stansfield enjoyed a purple patch, scoring six times in eight games in the autumn. Ryan Harley, with his priceless ability to strike the ball cleanly with either foot, scored several gems from distance, and Matt Gill kept popping up in the right place. When City secured their fourth successive

Matt Gill scores from the penalty spot against Darlington.

away win, at Barnet in late October, 986 fans went with them and Gill made it six goals in nine games, including four in four games during September.

'For someone who maybe knocks in two or three at the most every season, to score nine was brilliant for me,' said Gill, 'but I think that was down to Rob Edwards and the sort of formation we were playing. Rob gave me licence to get forward, knowing he was behind me. He is an excellent footballer and an excellent talker. He was my travelling partner from Bristol every day, so we became very close. It was my most enjoyable year and most successful on the pitch. It was an unbelievable season to be part of.'

Captains' Log

Exeter began the season with one centre-half, Danny Seaborne, as captain and ended it with another, Matt Taylor, wearing the armband. They joined a lengthy list during Paul Tisdale's time in charge, which also included Chris Todd, Matt Gill, Rob Edwards, George Friend, Andy Taylor and Dean Moxey.

'We've changed captains,' the manager said, 'but I'm neither embarrassed nor proud of the fact that we've had quite a few. Chris Todd was captain when I arrived and it seemed appropriate that he should continue. Then he moved on and Andy

Taylor was a very good role model within the club and played his part. Matt Gill was an obvious choice as someone who was going to play every week – he was clearly one of our most consistent performers, week in and week out. Dan Seaborne then came in and the captaincy became his when he came into the side because I thought it would enhance his performance, so it was as much what we could get out of it as he could get out of it, so that was a different slant.

'I guess the point is that there is no one theory, I'm not tied to one particular type, and also you don't have to wear the armband to be a captain. It's a fluid situation, and the most important influence is probably the senior player within the team, not necessarily the captain.

'There are captains who lead by example and there are captains who lead by voice and galvanising the team, on the pitch or off it. I think a captain needs to be someone who, 99 times out of 100, you are going to select, because if he is going to reflect the manager and take the ethics of the club on to the pitch then it is very important that he's playing!'

The Wheels Come Off

City made steady progress through October, reeling off five wins and two draws which culminated in

A bleak day at Curzon Ashton.

that extremely disciplined performance at Barnet. So it came as a rude shock three days later when Chesterfield visited St James Park and handed out a 6–1 thrashing. By any standards, four of the goals Exeter conceded that night were horrors, with individual mistakes and some suicidal passing around their own penalty area. So it says something for the equanimity in the club that the team lined up with exactly the same starting eleven against Chester on the first day of November and responded with a 2–0 win.

It may seem odd to identify a 6–1 home defeat as a key moment in a successful season, but it is often said that you find out more about yourself in adversity. Matt Gill, on whom the blame for one of the goals could be laid, said, 'Chesterfield was important because we didn't make much of it. People can get too low after heavy defeats like that, but because of the character Tis is, there wasn't too much of an inquest into it. I think that probably helped us. No one got too low, no one started arguing in the dressing room, it was one of those when you say, "Let's move on and put it right the next game." Which we did.'

Out of the Cup – Again

Curzon Ashton were playing in the Unibond League when City drew them in the first round of the FA Cup. They were almost 100 places below City in the league pyramid – an order of magnitude similar to the gap between Exeter and Manchester United in 2005. In the biggest turn-up of the round, City lost 3–2.

No matter that Curzon's goals came via a deflection, a wonder strike on the turn into the top corner and a breakaway, it was a humiliating moment. Suddenly the Cup didn't appear quite so magical, and Matt Gill once again lost his cool and was sent off.

Tisdale insisted that there was nothing deliberate about the team's shortcomings in knockout football. 'It has not been for the want of trying,' he said. 'It just hasn't happened in the cup competitions. We go into every game wanting to win, it is just an irony we've not had much luck in the cups when our League form has been good.'

Perhaps City used up all their good fortune in being paired with United, but their subsequent record is modest. During Tisdale's first three seasons in charge, they played 12 cup matches, in four competitions, winning five and losing seven. Although there were FA Cup victories over AFC Wimbledon, Ebbsfleet and Stevenage to enjoy, Stockport, Bury and Curzon ended City's interest in the most glamorous competition of them all. Meanwhile, when City returned to the League Cup in 2008, Southampton made their Championship status tell. The silver lining may have been that Exeter, unencumbered by cup competitions, made great strides in the League, particularly after Christmas. There may, however, be some supporters who would quite fancy a game against Arsenal, or even Wigan for that matter.

Subtle Changes

So with cup football out of the way for another year City were free to focus on League action – unfortunately, without Matt Taylor, their influential and combative centre-half, who injured his foot against Aldershot and missed the next nine games. Later in the season, he broke the fourth metatarsal – the curse of the modern-day footballer – in his right foot and missed another six games. Statistics show that Taylor was a big miss, even though Rob Edwards was able to slot back into the middle of defence, as clean sheets proved very hard to come by in his absence. 'Matt is a certain type of player that most teams require,' said Tisdale. 'He is wholehearted, brave and determined, and very good in the penalty boxes. He is first to the ball and likes to win it.'

Craig McAllister, meanwhile, had to wait until December for his first goal but scored it within 128 seconds of coming on as a substitute in the home win against Lincoln. The following week he again left the bench, this time to score twice against

Craig McAllister on the mark against Lincoln.

Rochdale. Exeter's 14-man game and the role of the goalscoring substitute was taking shape.

The year ended disappointingly, however, with a 2–0 home defeat by Brentford when Edwards was penalised for a perfect example of a sliding tackle with his 'wrong' right foot, giving Charlie MacDonald the opportunity to break the deadlock in a tight game from the penalty spot. And when City lost the first game of the new year at Notts County, an end was finally brought to a truly remarkable run of 120 games under Tisdale (and 125 in all for the club) of not suffering back-to-back League defeats. As well as being an obviously resilient outfit, the Grecians also had a habit of getting stronger in the second half of a season, which augured well.

Aiming High

Just when did automatic promotion become a realistic aim for Exeter following their return to the Football League? Most teams that come up via the play-offs, as City had, are happy to occupy a position in the middle of the table; most find they have enough momentum to survive comfortably. The more optimistic City fan might have argued that, having missed out on promotion in 2007, City's players had grown stronger, wiser and a little older during their final year in the Conference and were better prepared to soar through the higher division rather than just make up the numbers.

The lack of activity during January's transfer window certainly helped. Exeter began the new year in seventh place and with a growing reputation for playing attractive, passing football and for having a clutch of promising young players – an irresistible combination for scouts from Championship clubs.

Paul Tisdale's adage is that 'more bad decisions than good ones are made in January', but the month passed with Paul Jones, Dean Moxey and Matt Gill still in harness and Exeter in good shape to look to start closing the 10-point gap which Wycombe, the division leaders, had opened up.

For Tisdale and most of the players, League Two was a learning curve, though not as steep as some might have suspected. So when did the manager believe the team had what it took to do well in the division, maybe even make a serious push for promotion? 'When's the cut-off point? After 10 games, a dozen games? Logic tells you it's when you've played everyone else once. At what point did we think we were up to the league? Was it when we went to Bradford and got hammered 4–1? No. We needed a lot more gumption in the side to go through those kind of days without getting beat heavily. At what point did I think we had half a chance? Our football during the period when we had some really good away wins, including Port Vale and Barnet in the space of a few days, was of a really good level.

'Success is made up of so many intangibles. Some parts you can only really feel. Has the team got the gumption, the determination to drive through the disappointments? No game is perfect, you don't always get the run of the ball or the decisions, and you have to have enough about you that, whatever the situation, you come out on top. I would say we began to get that resolution in February time, and I thought we had a chance.'

Dagenham, a Turning Point

Exeter had gone to Dagenham on 13 December for what appeared a routine game between two

Troy Archibald-Henville.

'It was vital for us, that signing, because I knew we needed to toughen up a little bit in that sort of position. We changed our system to three at the back to freshen things up and it gave us that extra strength in the back line. Dagenham was a real tough game. It was big because we recognised an escape from a game we were losing. In life, when you get a second chance, you've got to take it.

'We could have let it pass us by, but we were not the sort of team to allow that to happen, so it became a real focus for us over quite a few weeks that that game was going to be a turning point, and I think we knew we were going to win it. Most of the time it is about recognising a moment to capitalise, so we built up to it, to make the point that this is where we freshen things up and this is the start of the second half of the season.'

top-half sides in League Two. It proved anything but. Trailing 1–0 to a goal by Paul Benson and looking out of sorts, City played out the last 10 minutes before half-time in an eerie gloom after the floodlights failed. After an unusually lengthy interval, the game was called off.

By the time it was replayed, on 20 January, Exeter had a new addition to the ranks, and they won thanks to two goals from Craig McAllister, who was starting for the first time.

If the result seemed like a stroke of good fortune, the recruitment of 6ft 2in Troy Archibald-Henville, on loan from Tottenham, at what seemed like a moment's notice to combat the usual aerial bombardment served up by the East London side, said much about Exeter's meticulous preparation.

Archibald-Henville had arrived at the Cat & Fiddle in early December and spent two weeks at the club before heading back to Spurs. So although he was signed at the last minute, it was not the gamble it appeared, although switching formations at Dagenham brought a degree of risk.

Tisdale said, 'We knew we needed real cover for Dan Seaborne and Matt Taylor. Part of the reason for not wanting loans is that you are guessing. It's a rabbit out of a hat sometimes and I like considered opinions and a pragmatic approach, but the fact that we had the knowledge of Alex Inglethorpe at Spurs, which was vital to it, and the fact that we were able to have the player in to spend some time with us, took out some of the variables. It wasn't about his ability, it was about how he was as a person, how he liked it down here and whether he would fit into our style of play.

Troy Archibald-Henville may not be the biggest name in English football yet, but he can certainly lay claim to being the longest. Not since Forbes Phillipson-Masters donned the red and white in the 1970s have Exeter had such an exotically monickered player, and in those days there were no names on the backs of shirts.

When Exeter signed Archibald-Henville on loan from Tottenham in something of a hurry to play against Dagenham, it gave City kit man Shaun Hayward a king-sized headache, with 18 characters to squeeze on to the back of the new signing's shirt. City asked the Football League whether 'Troy' would be acceptable but they refused, so Hayward took delivery of a hastily prepared 'iron on' strip containing the Archibald-Henville name, but even that was wrong. Normally, the letters are curved to fit neatly around the number on the back of a shirt, but these were firmly arranged in a straight line.

Troy made a winning start to his City career but even he was forced to admit that, with fans having to pay for each letter, there was unlikely to be much demand for Archibald-Henville replica shirts. However, if ever a name lent itself to a fans' chant, then his is surely it. By the time City played at Gillingham four days later, the songsmiths had been at work on that six-syllable name and he appeared to have half a dozen tunes, though woe betide anyone who yelled, 'Give us a T, give us an R...'

Formations

A change in formation, whether at the start of the game or during the 90 minutes, can work wonders for a team, but it also has profound consequences for the players – especially if they find their position doesn't exist any more in the new set-up.

For defender Steve Tully, the switch to three at the back meant expanding his repertoire. 'When I was at Weymouth, I played sweeper, so when Tis said he was thinking of changing formation I thought, Great, perhaps I will play sweeper again. But when he pulled me in he said he saw me as more of a right-side centre-half because he thought I could attack almost like a right-back when we had the ball, and in fact the more I played it the more I enjoyed it. You are always looking to develop as a player and trying different formations seemed to work for me and gave the manager another option.

'I do pride myself on not being a sitting, boring right-back, because I do like to bomb on every chance I get. One thing I have had to develop under Tis is my defensive side, and he's helped me out loads. I feel I know my position inside out now and I'm more comfortable and I pace myself during the game. I still feel I'm improving under him and that's down to the manager.

'He has always impressed on us the need to get the ball down and play, and we surprised a lot of teams, especially early in the season, with the way we played, but he's not afraid to change if need be. For instance, we started out the season playing 4-4-2, then went to 4-3-3 before ending the season playing 3-5-2. After Christmas, teams started changing their formations to play us, which is the biggest compliment of all.'

Russell and Fleetwood

A rather more successful combination in the history of Exeter City than the infamous Russell and Lewis, Alex Russell and Stuart Fleetwood were signed as the games came thick and fast in the spring of 2009. Russell, an experienced midfielder, came from Cheltenham, while Fleetwood was signed on loan from Charlton. Russell succumbed to injury after seven games, so with Adam Stansfield and Marcus Stewart also limping out of contention before the end of the season the arrival of Fleetwood and his red boots proved a masterstroke.

Explaining the decision to sign Fleetwood, a prolific goalscorer in the Conference for Forest Green Rovers but unable to make an impression at Charlton, Tisdale said, 'We had had a real good first half of the season playing Adam Stansfield largely on his own, and I didn't think he could just carry on on his own. There is also the second-time-around scenario that people knew him, so I thought, Let's change it a bit and have two of them up front – two first-class runners. It was timed almost to the second for the last 12 games of the season, to give Adam a partner up there. Stuart was a forceful character in terms of his optimism and his confidence – goalscorers tend to be, and he's a goalscorer.'

Fleetwood had a couple of sighters as a substitute before finding his range in spectacular fashion against Dagenham in a 2–1 home win. If the first – six touches, two changes of direction and a 20-yard curling finish – was beautifully crafted, the second bore the hallmark of a true goalscorer: the ability to fashion a goal out of virtually nothing. Receiving a Matt Gill throw on the corner of the penalty area, Fleetwood allowed the ball to bounce across his body as he turned towards goal, and just before it hit the ground he made perfect contact with his right foot and sent the ball soaring 20 yards or more into the far top corner. The Dagenham goalkeeper was just a spectator.

Both were contenders for City's goal of the season, but there were numerous others: Liam Sercombe's interception, dribble and looping left-foot finish at Port Vale; Dean Moxey's chest control and ferocious half-volley in a losing cause at Curzon Ashton; Manny Panther's change of feet and left-foot curler at Morecambe; Moxey's 25-yard rocket following a short free kick with Ryan Harley at Chesterfield; Neil Saunders's 35-yard lob volley against Barnet when the ball didn't touch the ground between Paul Jones's feet (via Marcus Stewart's header) and the back of the net. A personal favourite would be Stewart rolling back the years at Grimsby, controlling Moxey's sweeping free kick, cutting back inside a covering defender and bending a 20-yard shot into the top corner.

The Run-in

On Easter weekend, Exeter travelled to Brentford. Or rather the fans took over Brentford, as 1,800 of them filled the two-tier stand at the away end and made a fearful din as the team were bombarded by Andy Scott's League leaders.

Then Stuart Fleetwood did it again. Manny Panther won the ball, Ryan Harley unlocked the defence and Fleetwood's quick feet carried him inside one challenge for a clinical finish.

City fans fill the away end at Brentford.

It was backs-to-the-wall stuff, and City owed Brentford for their streaky victory at St James Park in December. It looked as if they might gain revenge, and three supremely important points, when Paul Jones saved a penalty from Billy Clarke, awarded for a handball by Matt Gill, but Clarke popped up in the 90th minute to equalise.

A point gained or two points lost? It was difficult to say. City were fourth, with four to play, and so many of the top teams had still to play one another. The permutations were virtually endless, but if one thing was certain it was that the promotion race would go all the way to Rotherham on the last day of the season.

Victory against Wycombe two days later, on Easter Monday, was a huge result, but Wycombe still had a game in hand. The greater threat to achieving a top-three finish seemed to come from Bury, Rochdale and Gillingham. Gill scored the solitary goal against Wycombe, from the tightest of angles in front of a packed home end at St James Park. 'It was tight but I thought I had nothing to lose,' he said. 'Ryan Harley played a long diagonal ball, it dropped to me on the volley and I just thought I'd have a swing at it, and it managed to creep in between the keeper and the

near post. It was nice seeing that go in on the TV replays in the bar after the game.'

Three to go, and victory at Lincoln was secured with Dean Moxey's 'goal' in added time, a huge inswinger that curled across the penalty area, clipped the far post and bounced into the net off the back of the goalkeeper. Lucky? Maybe, but the boy had form dating back to Doncaster Rovers all those years ago.

A week later, Morecambe at home was a nerve-racking affair. Even victory wouldn't have guaranteed promotion, but City had to settle for a 2–2 draw in front of 8,544 fans. City scored two superb goals, through Moxey and Harley, but were undone by Morecambe's prowess at set-pieces.

Whatever happened now, the team had shown incredible strength of character and resilience. After defeat at Chesterfield on 28 January City were in 10th place with 19 League games remaining. As the goal of promotion came increasingly into focus and other teams lost their nerve, City barely wavered. They failed to score only once (in a goalless draw at Chester), they scored late goals, they recovered from going behind to draw or win, they won at home against Port Vale after playing for 70 minutes with 10 men

Stuart Fleetwood weaves his way into the Brentford area to score.

Relief as Dean Moxey equalises in the final home game against Morecambe.

following Danny Seaborne's sending-off, and they accumulated a phenomenal 39 points from those 19 games. The question was whether that was going to be enough for automatic promotion or a third successive year in the play-offs, which now seemed an increasingly unappealing prospect.

City fans whip up an atmosphere in Sheffield.

Sheffield is one of Britain's great footballing cities and boasts two historic, atmospheric grounds. Unfortunately, the Don Valley Stadium is not one of them.

When Exeter fans arrived in Sheffield city centre on Saturday 2 May, it was not for a short walk to Sheffield United's Bramall Lane, or a trip north to Hillsborough, home to Wednesday and host to so many FA Cup semi-finals until the tragedy in 1989 that bears its name. Instead, the West Country hordes joined the trams heading east, which were already full of shoppers apparently oblivious to the drama about to unfold on their doorstep, interested only in the delights of the Meadowhall shopping centre, two stops further on.

City's supporters were heading for undoubtedly the least atmospheric ground in the Football League, a vast open site with only one grandstand, running the length of one side of the pitch. As a venue for one of the most important days in the club's history, it could hardly have been less prepossessing. The solitary bar could not begin to cope, and wherever one sat the view was of open spaces. In the middle, surrounded by an athletics track, was a pitch which even at a distance seemed dry and uneven.

Yet this was not the least of the team's problems. Rotherham may have begun the season with a 17-point deduction, but unlike Luton Town – whose 30-point penalty had dragged them down into the Conference – the Millers had turned adversity into a surprisingly successful season. Despite finding themselves playing in the wastelands of Sheffield's outskirts after a dispute with the owners of Millmoor, their traditional home, Mark Robins's team had prospered. So much so that, but for the deduction, they would have started the day only a point behind Exeter. They were even collecting a trophy, from Sky's *Soccer AM* programme, for winning League 2A, open only to those who began the season with points deductions.

Although there was nothing in it for their team, the Rotherham supporters had turned up in surprisingly large numbers for the final game of the season. To add spice to the mix, Robins and Paul Tisdale had been team-mates 10 years earlier at Panionios in Greece.

The arithmetic remained the same, though: City needed to match anything fourth-placed Bury could achieve against Accrington to guarantee promotion. But the ground, the supporters, that pitch and a more than decent opposition confirmed what everyone had known all along: this

Rob Edwards takes a throw with the massed ranks of City fans behind him.

was the toughest assignment for any of the top four clubs that day.

The Set-up

After 45 games, almost 11,000 miles and a host of lows and, mostly, highs, it all came down to these 90 minutes. It had to be a collective effort. Striker Richard Logan, who began the match as a substitute, said, 'The manager said before the game it was the last time we would all be in the room together, so we would walk out together as a squad.'

'That was the premise of the day,' Tisdale confirmed. 'You can't talk about every variable going into a game. You've got to pick something, whether it's a tactic or a mood. There was a definite tactic for that game, but you can't have a big tactic for every game of the season, the players would go mad. You've got to wait for when it's needed. We've had play-off games, the Dagenham game, when you really go for something and you seize the occasion. So there's a tactic involved and there's a mood. The mood that day, I decided, was that while the players were focusing on the game, I wanted to remind everyone that it was the last time they would all be in that room together.

'We had gone through all this work together all year, on the coaches for hours, on the training ground. We had fought together, we had argued together, and now we had a chance to create a little bit of history. But this would be the last time we would all be together as a group. It's quite inspiring. Win, lose or draw, it was a case of saying, "Come on. You might be best friends with your playing mate or he might irritate you, but actually, in 20 years' time, you'll look back and you played with this chap all year." It was just jumping on a bit of a mood.'

The Reality

'We were quite happy it was away, actually,' said Tisdale, 'and to get away from the pressure of St James Park. The last game there, the Morecambe game, was hideous. The expectation was almost unbearable and I am glad we came out with a draw – that was a terrific result. This was a simpler game for us and I preferred it that way round.

'We knew Rotherham weren't playing for anything but that they were a very good team who would have been right up there if it hadn't been for the points deduction. We knew it was a tough game and the pitch wasn't perfect, but I don't mind that stadium. I spent seven years at Team Bath playing inside a running track and I had played on that pitch for Huddersfield reserves and scored a very good goal, so I liked that place and the supporters made it a great atmosphere. It was great being out there and looking at the crowd. It was different for them looking back past us and seeing nothing, but I really enjoyed that day. I liked the set-up. Supporters might have a different view but we had a clear picture.

'There was nothing clever about it other than that we were focused. It was a difficult, difficult game, but ultimately it could have been anybody. Look how much Bury struggled at home against Accrington.'

A Player's View

For many of the Exeter players, this was the third successive year of playing what was effectively a cup final, and the experience was invaluable. Defender Steve Tully said his team-mates did indeed have a clear image of what was required at Rotherham. 'It was almost like a downer after the Morecambe game, but then it was back to business and we knew what we had to do. Tis said on the Monday morning that we had a job to do, it was in our hands, and that's the way we would have wanted it. He said it was down to us. We would play a certain way and it would suit us, and to believe in him. If we believed in each other, like we had all season, then we would go up there and get a result.

'It was a really good week. Monday, work on a few things; Tuesday, work a bit on fitness and a bit of running; Wednesday, off; in on Thursday, as

Bertie Cozic in the thick of the action.

Dean Moxey strikes for goal.

normal; then set off on the road on Friday. When we got there, everyone looked at the pitch and said, "Oh my God, we should be doing track and field here, not playing football on it." There were divots, javelin marks, but they had to play on it every week. But as soon as you come out to warm up and see thousands of our fans, you just think, Yes, we are here to do a job, let's just get on and do it.'

The League Table at 3 p.m.

Brentford	P45 Pts 82 GD 27
Wycombe	P45 Pts 78 GD 22
Exeter	**P45 Pts 76 GD 14**
Bury	P45 Pts 75 GD 19

The Game

Rotherham United 0 Exeter City 1 (Logan 71)

Rotherham United: Warrington; Tonge, Sharps, Fenton, Green; Harrison, Mills, Hudson (J. Taylor 81), R. Taylor; Broughton (Burchill 72), Reid (Brogan 85). Subs: Cann (g), Holmes.
Sent off: Tonge.

Exeter City: Jones; Tully, M. Taylor, Archibald-Henville, Edwards; Sercombe (Logan 61), Cozic (McAllister 61), Gill, Harley, Moxey; Fleetwood (Basham 85).
Subs: Marriott (g), Seaborne.

Referee: P. Taylor

Attendance: 6,184

It is easy to talk about destiny and plans coming to fruition after the event, but Exeter's game at Rotherham was quintessential Exeter City and Paul Tisdale. It was about meticulous planning, a smart strategy – brilliantly executed – some outstanding individual performances, but above all it was a team effort.

Of course the day wasn't just about what was happening in Sheffield, but about events at Bury and at Wycombe, who were at home to Accrington and Notts County respectively.

Exeter's vast travelling army had a very poor view of the action but they could see clearly enough when Troy Archibald-Henville cleared a shot from Drewe Broughton off the line after the Rotherham striker had lifted the ball over Paul Jones. At the other end, Stuart Fleetwood missed his kick and then shot over, while Matt Taylor headed straight at the goalkeeper.

At half-time, the top of the table was unchanged. Wycombe were losing to a long-range shot from Notts County's John Thompson and Bury were still goalless against Accrington. However, within a minute of the restarts around the country, Accrington were awarded a penalty, which might have been enough to put Bury out of the reckoning. Except that Peter Cavanagh hit the crossbar. And then Wycombe equalised. It was back to square one, which meant Exeter had to win to make sure. If Bury scored now, City would be down to fourth.

Rather than hang on and hope for assistance from elsewhere, Tisdale sent on Craig McAllister and Richard Logan and changed the shape of the team. Instead of 4-5-1, with Fleetwood as a lone striker, Rotherham now had three forwards to contend with. The ball began to flow with increasing regularity towards the home goal and

Richard Logan climbs highest at the far post to head Exeter in front.

the expectant, twitchy City fans, and McAllister forced two saves.

Then it happened. A short corner, Ryan Harley to Rob Edwards, back to Harley, back to Edwards, the glance up, the long cross beyond the far post and the 6ft 1in Logan outjumping 5ft 7in Jamie Green to head the ball past Andy Warrington. The same Andy Warrington who was outwitted by Dean Moxey's 45-yard shot against Doncaster in the FA Cup all those years earlier. Deliriously, Logan turned and ran back down the touchline in front of the main stand, for reasons that were not immediately apparent.

Now it began to seem like destiny, and when Rotherham defender Dale Tonge was sent off for a cynical foul on McAllister it looked as if it might be ecstasy as well. Except that, for the sixth time during the season, City failed from the penalty spot as Warrington dived to his left to save Fleetwood's shot.

Delight for the supporters.

Fleetwood headed for the bench to wonder just how costly his miss might prove, but City's nerve did not fail, even if Wycombe's did. They conceded another goal, in the 90th minute, to John Thompson, and had to wait five minutes for the result from Bury.

The Lancashire team did win in the end, thanks, almost inevitably, to yet another penalty, followed by a pitch invasion which held the game up for several minutes. One more goal and they would have gone up on goal difference at Wycombe's expense. But Exeter were in the clear. The whistle sounded, they were promoted for a second successive year, and the celebrations could really begin.

The League Table at 5 p.m.

Brentford	P46 Pts 85 GD 29
Exeter	**P46 Pts 79 GD 15**
Wycombe	P46 Pts 78 GD 21
Bury	P46 Pts 78 GD 20

Events Elsewhere

'Steve Perryman was on the phone and we had someone at Bury,' said Paul Tisdale, 'but the players had decided they didn't want to know what was happening and they wanted to win the game, which I think was symptomatic of a very focused, determined team. So, yes, we did know, but it was irrelevant because the players didn't want to know – they just wanted to win.'

Remaining Calm

'Even at half-time,' said Steve Tully, 'when it was nil-nil, I looked around and could see that everyone in the changing room had that inner belief that we were going to do it. I never thought they would win the game, and as soon as they went down to 10 men, I thought, The game's over, we've just got to see it out. We had a game plan, we stuck to it, and it worked. The one thing Tis said at half-time was that we were creating chances – he would have been worried if we weren't – and just to be patient and one would come.'

The Winning Tactic

Exeter's management team had been at the Don Valley Stadium 11 days earlier to watch Rotherham

Stuart Fleetwood misses from the penalty spot.

than if you'd not had it. There's a psychological hurt to missing, and it boosts the other side. If you'd asked me that split-second about having a penalty or not, I'd probably rather not, because I could sense that if we did miss it there might be a problem.'

There were times during the season when it seemed Exeter couldn't play a game without conceding or being awarded a penalty, or, as was the case at Rochdale, both teams being awarded one in little over a minute.

In all, there were more penalties in Exeter games (20) than for any other team in the division – 10 for City and 10 for their opponents. It takes a brave man to step up and take a penalty but, unfortunately, all the City takers – with one notable exception – proved fallible from 12 yards:

Chester (h) Logan – saved
Rotherham (h) Watson – saved
Rochdale (h) Basham – scored
Notts County (a) Stewart – scored
Dagenham (a) McAllister – saved, but scored from rebound
Chesterfield (a) Basham – saved
Darlington (h) Gill – scored
Shrewsbury (a) Gill – hit crossbar
Rochdale (a) Stewart – scored
Rotherham (a) Fleetwood – saved

Thank goodness for Paul Jones. The man who saved a penalty with his first touch as an Exeter player, and in his first appearance at Wembley, saved four of the 10 he faced, and got a hand to several more. The saves at home to Barnet and at Brentford alone garnered three extra points, courtesy of the anticipation of the fans' player of the year.

Conclusion: if Marcus Stewart had taken all the penalties, Exeter would have been promoted as champions before the end of April.

play Morecambe. Steve Perryman said, 'At the end, Paul turned to me and said, "They are weak on the back post."'

'The thing with set-pieces,' Tisdale explained, 'is that you can't cover everything and there is one weakness somewhere in any set-piece. It's about patience, it's about quality, and it's about having the right people doing the right jobs.

'Ryan Harley and Rob Edwards had the ability and the composure just to take their time and put up with that "Get it in the box!" from 2,500 people and just create that bit more space at the back post, and Logie came in. It had to be Logie, didn't it?'

The Penalty

Shortly after Stuart Fleetwood missed from the penalty spot, he was substituted. 'I couldn't bear to watch the last 10 minutes from the bench,' he said. Then again, he was scarcely the first Exeter player to err from the spot.

'I wasn't overly confident because we had had a shocking season of penalties,' Tisdale said. 'Did I know what would happen? I thought it was fifty-fifty – I was just philosophical about it. I probably would have preferred not to have had the penalty, because through missing it you actually feel worse

The Goalscorer

A year earlier, Richard Logan had scored the goal that sank Torquay in the play-offs. At Sheffield, he was primed for a repeat. 'Tis said at half-time, "You are going to come on and change the game

John Yems and Paul Tisdale at the final whistle.

Steve Tully celebrates.

Tears of joy on the terraces.

or get a goal and be a hero," and that's how it worked out.

'Macca and I were practising getting on the end of diagonal balls at half-time, before we came on. When we got the corner, I was hoping they would put it in the box and I could get across my man. Usually I hang around at the back a lot, and during the week Tis kept telling me "Just keep getting across the man", and I just managed to do that and headed it in.

'I completely forgot about the fans because I had said that if I scored I was going to go to the lads who weren't involved, like Neil Saunders and Manny Panther, who were sitting in the main stand with my brother, Stewart, because they were all part of it and I wanted to celebrate with them.

'Torquay was a great occasion, but getting the goal to get us promotion tops that. It was a special moment, and it's definitely the goal that has meant the most to me.

'I have a great relationship with the fans. I would like to play more, but in the big games I seem to

Promotion party in the dressing room.

come up with the goods. The fans always chant my name, and if I'm out walking in town with my little one they are always stopping me to talk.

'I played England under-15s up to under-20s with Jermain Defoe and he's at the other end of the scale now, playing for Spurs and England. Maybe I let myself go a bit when I was younger and enjoyed life too much, thinking I had already made it, but I'm settled now and I've got some great memories here.'

The Opposing Manager

With about 30 seconds to go, in a break with normal protocol, Mark Robins walked across to the Exeter bench and shook Paul Tisdale's hand. 'I thought it was a really nice touch on his part,' said the Exeter manager. 'I've seen him since but I remember thinking at the time that it was a really good thing to do. We spent a year together in Athens and I go back to that team thing. You spend a lot of time with people and I think that really does accentuate a relationship when you are team-mates living abroad. I get on really well with Mark. I don't think he was conceding the game, I think he recognised that we were going to have a celebration and wanted to say "Well done" before he lost his opportunity.'

'I was pleased for Paul,' Robins said, 'because he's done a remarkable job down there to re-establish Exeter as a football club. I remember looking at the job when it became available – before he took it – and they were talking about working with a football trust and I know that can be difficult, but he is certainly the type of person who can do that and be successful. I was delighted for him, although I was disappointed we had lost the game. Even at the end of a long season he had his game plan, he stuck to it, and it came off, but that's what he's like. He tries to out-think other people and sticks to it and he has got his rewards for it.'

It Starts to Sink in

Goalkeeper Paul Jones, the only ever-present in the team, was voted the fans' player of the year but was quick to share the praise. 'I began the season with the aim of playing every game. I'm not a fan of personal awards because it's a team game and the whole team deserve one. I think promotion was better than Wembley. Wembley is a good day out, but to go up and finish second against stronger teams in your first season is an unbelievable achievement.'

Captain Matt Taylor, who played the final three

The manager gets a soaking.

games through the pain of his recent metatarsal operation, said, 'Five years ago I was playing in goal in non-League football, and look at where I am now.'

A False Start for the Promotion Party

The instant the final whistle sounded, a phalanx of South Yorkshire police officers formed a physical barrier across the pitch, which seemed a slight over-reaction given that the Exeter fans appeared in no hurry to ignore instructions not to encroach on to the running track that surrounded the pitch.

In fact, the police were more concerned with keeping an unruly element among the home support in check, but it meant that little was seen of the Exeter players by the fans, many of whom wandered down on to the running track, although Dean Moxey conspicuously wanted to share the moment with his family.

So there was to be no salute – that would have to wait for an open-top bus tour through the streets of Exeter a week later – and eventually the supporters drifted away to celebrate in Sheffield while the players and staff marked the occasion as best they could in an under-resourced athletics

stadium. 'We hadn't planned anything,' Paul Tisdale said, 'and I was conscious that we shouldn't. One of the few things I didn't plan last year was if we got promoted. I planned everything else but not that, so we didn't really know what to do.

'It was disappointing in a way that the police asked us to move off the pitch because I think it deprived our supporters of a really special moment – or at least the chance to extend that special moment. We were told to come off the pitch, so we went to the dressing room and had a bit of a party and the players started to get showered, and then the police came back in and said, "You can go back out now," but it was too late by then, which was a real shame, because the moment had gone and half the players were showered and half weren't and the supporters had started to drift away. But in the grand scheme of things, whether it was 10 minutes or 10 hours, it was a special moment.

'The players then got on the coach, but I had a lot of press interviews to do so they gave up and got off again and went to the bar and waited for me to finish all the interviews, which took about an hour and a half. Then we did finally get on the coach and had a sing-song all the way home. I've not heard, before or since, our players have a sing-song, but they did that day, and it was a very special five- or six-hour journey.

'It was different from Wembley in 2008 because that day everyone had family there and went their own way, so there were only about 10 of us on the coach home, which was a really strange situation. The previous year, when we had lost there, we were all on the coach and we all sat depressed together. The second year, everyone was fearing the worst and they had all decided to make their own arrangements, just in case we lost, so it was very quiet. Rotherham was special because the whole squad had a really special few hours together that you rarely get in football.'

Well done, son: Paul Tisdale and his father, Robert.

Exeter High Street on the day of the victory parade.

An early working sub-title for this book was 'From Northwich to Norwich in two glorious years,' which was rightly rejected as too obscure, but did have the merit of summing up the extent of the journey Exeter City made between August 2007 and May 2009. Instead of finding Forest Green Rovers and Histon on the fixture list, City could look forward to Charlton Athletic, Leeds United, Southampton and Norwich – all recently of the Premier League.

Even as Exeter's players and staff enjoyed a richly deserved victory parade aboard an open-top bus through the city centre, followed by a reception at the Guildhall hosted by the Lord Mayor, the nagging doubt of what awaited them in League One, and the fact that football never stands still for a moment, must have been at the back of more than a few minds.

The players then enjoyed a celebration party back at St James Park, when Matt Gill was named

player of the year by the rest of the squad, but as Paul Tisdale had pointed out on the eve of the Rotherham game, change was inevitable and Gill became the first player to move on when he signed for Norwich.

Before that, though, there were accolades to be collected as well as air to be walked on by City fans all over the world. Tisdale won the LMA (League Managers Association) Coca-Cola League Two manager of the year, voted for by his peers and presented by Terry Venables. He also won the Orange 2008/09 Manager of the Year award when, after 330,000 discerning votes from members of the public, the 1-2-3 was Paul Tisdale, Owen Coyle (Burnley) and Fabio Capello, the England manager. Sir Alex Ferguson was in 14th place.

A sure sign of the growing profile of club and manager came when Tisdale was asked by Radio 5 Live to provide analysis for the League Two play-

Exeter City's promotion squad 2009.

off final at Wembley, where at half-time he neatly dissected the tactical approaches of the winners, Gillingham, and Shrewsbury.

For Tisdale, a summer without play-offs meant more time with his family but also making a start on earning his Uefa Pro Licence, the highest award and a pre-requisite for anyone to manage in Europe's top divisions. 'I am on the last step now. It's taken a while to get there and it has been hard,' he said. 'A lot of players leave it until they finish playing because it's difficult to fit it all in. Through circumstance, I've started very early. At 36, when most players are starting to think about it, I've had 10 years and that's an advantage.'

Inevitably, with two promotions on his CV, Tisdale was linked with a host of jobs during the close season. Whatever the appeal of Reading, Swansea or Southampton, with its obvious emotional resonance, the most significant story of a summer of changing personnel at Exeter turned out to be a non-story and Tisdale was very much in charge when the fixture list was released on 17 June 2009. And what a fixture list. The first game of the season would take Exeter to Elland Road, Leeds – to a club where the record signing was £18 million spent on Rio Ferdinand. Exeter's record was still the £65,000 they had paid for Tony Kellow way

back in March 1980, yet they would arrive as equals – in league status, at any rate.

Should I Stay or Should I Go?

Marcus Stewart, one short of his 250th career goal, put off retirement for another year. 'When I came to Exeter I wasn't sure what it was going to be like but I soon realised how well the club is run and it gave me a bit of a cause to carry on,' he said. 'I really enjoyed last season and training has been first class. I genuinely think Paul Tisdale is a top person and a top manager and I have enjoyed working with him. If it wasn't for him, I would probably have retired by now.'

For Gill, though, the lure of Norwich proved irresistible. 'I spoke to Tis in the summer and said it would be very hard to leave for any other club. There were rumours about Wycombe and others but I would always like to think that I would have stayed at Exeter if it wasn't for Norwich. To go and play for your home-town club was an opportunity I couldn't miss really.'

Steve Perryman paid tribute to Gill, the midfield heartbeat of the two promotion teams. 'We have been good for each other. He helped us to two promotions and was probably one of the top players in the Conference and then in League Two. Now he has decided to go back to his roots and we would like to thank him for his tremendous contribution to the club.'

Dean Moxey's departure was more protracted but Nigel Clough knew from his Burton Albion days how useful an acquisition he would be for Derby and eventually raised his opening offer of £200,000 to £350,000. It was good business and a tribute to the club's youth development, but to those who had watched Moxey mature into an outstanding footballer it still felt like the end of an era.

For Tisdale, there were mixed feelings: 'Am I sad to see Dean go? Yes, I am desperately disappointed, in the same way that I was to see George Friend and Jamie Mackie go. But we can be proud of the fact that players are benefiting from the way we are playing our football and the progress we are making. We are benefiting off the back of their performances, so it is a two-way street but Dean has been outstanding and thoroughly deserves his move to that level.'

Playing the Game

Players' contracts habitually run from July 1 to June 30, and so, as the club weighed up potential new recruits, there is a natural break at which this part of the story should end. It is worth noting, however, that the principles Tisdale found when he arrived at the club, of winning the right way and of fair play, were written through the previous seasons like 'Brighton' through a stick of rock. The team's passing game won plaudits from all quarters and, even in the heat of promotion to League One, Exeter had the fourth best disciplinary record in the country and came close to winning the Bobby Moore Fair Play award.

Steve Perryman said: 'Fair play doesn't mean play soft or play weak, it just means play the ball. We try not to pick up unnecessary bookings and that attitude has contributed to our success.' It certainly made a welcome change from the perennial trips to the FA in days gone by to explain away a dreadful disciplinary record, and appeared to reflect a culture within the club which expected players to act maturely.

'I have never fined a player a penny in three-and-bit years at Exeter City,' said Tisdale, 'yet we were top of the fair play twice in the Conference and then fourth in whole Football League. I don't think you have to fine players for being late to the bus, you have to manage them. You have to make them

understand how they have let the side down. One day I will fine someone but you can have good discipline by making people have responsibility and ownership of their part of a team that wants to achieve something.'

The reorganisation of the playing and coaching staff continued apace and a record number of City fans bought season tickets in anticipation of who knows what adventures in League One. A day will come, though it is to be hoped it is a long way off, when none of the promotion team of 2009 remains at the club and when Exeter may once again face hard times, though heaven forbid as hard as they were in 2003. That is the compelling nature of football and why supporting a team stirs such emotions. But for those who were there – whether players, staff or supporters – we will always have Rotherham.

The View from the Touchline

Everywhere Exeter City go, a hardy bunch of reporters follows. Of all the times to start, Matt Bamsey began covering the fortunes of Exeter City for the *Express and Echo* in the summer of 2003. It was a baptism of fire and over the next six years he missed only a handful of the club's 300-odd matches.

'I had been a news reporter before but it made it more of a challenge having to not only report on the football but also on how the club hauled themselves back from financial oblivion.

'The grimmest game I can remember was at Northwich Victoria on a Tuesday night when I was so cold I couldn't type and the dictaphone froze. The win over Cambridge at Wembley, after five years in the non-league doldrums, felt like the start of the good times, really. Everyone wanted to get out of the Conference so badly and I think it was a massive weight off all their shoulders – not just the players, but everyone who had worked so hard for the club.

'Just to be back in the Football League was enough, so going up to Rotherham looking for back-to-back promotions was almost beyond anyone's wildest dreams – a total bonus. Yet you very much got the sense that it was a chance to build on all that good work.

'Of all the people I have interviewed, Sean Devine – our last out-and-out goalscorer – was great copy. He was brutally honest and always told it how it was, but as a club I have always found the players very approachable.'

In its three years and various guises, *Kellow's*

Matt Bamsey.　　*Fullsy, Logie, Kirky.*

Bootlaces has become something of an Exeter City institution, first on internet radio, then local radio, and now as a fully fledged, and award-winning, internet show. Rooted firmly in the *Fantasy Football* tradition, Graham 'Kirky' Kirk and Barry 'Fullsy' Fulls have secured some wonderful scoops and deservedly won the EDF Energy South West media website of the year, although they insist it has been a collaborative effort.

Fulls said, 'The show would be nothing without the club's co-operation but I think the lesson for us is never be afraid to ask. To get someone like Ade Edmondson to give up his time and appear on the show was brilliant and probably the funniest interview I have ever been involved in. Phil Neal won nine championships with Liverpool and he came on our show. It's incredible.

'Another highlight would be after we won promotion for the second time when Dean Moxey and Bertie Cozic came into the studio to 'host' the show, which was a riot. We have had great access to Paul Tisdale, and John Yems was great – a naturally funny guy who was always happy to do an interview.'

Exeter City's programme, *The Grecian,* is a regular award winner, including the best in League Two for 2009 from *Programme Monthly* magazine. Under Mike Blackstone's editorship it has almost trebled in length since he took over in 1992. However, the internet revolution has changed the landscape in the way a club can communicate with their fans and the official website, *exetercityfc.co.uk,* has seen a huge growth in traffic. By the summer of 2009 it could boast almost half a million page views per month,

47,000 different users and, for a small fee, video footage and interviews on Grecian Player to complement the traditional match reports.

The site really made its mark before the Rotherham game when Peter Evans, the editor, published good luck messages from supporters and then passed them on to the team. The response to Exeter's victory in Yorkshire was even more memorable. 'My inbox was inundated with congratulations from ecstatic fans from around the globe, and we published them all,' said Evans. 'The response was phenomenal. To find over 100 emails in my inbox on that Sunday morning, from Plymouth to Perth, Western Australia, highlighted just what back-to-back promotions meant for Exeter.'

The social networking boom has added another dimension to the link between club and supporters and by July 2009 there were 3,500 fans of Exeter City on Facebook and almost 400 followers on Twitter. Nor will it stop there. 'We are launching a series of fan blogs on the website,' Evans said. 'We want our supporters to be able to share their views on their football club.'

The Legends

Alan Banks scored a century of goals in two spells for Exeter, between 1963 and 1973, and in 2007 he topped a poll of City's all-time favourite players conducted by the PFA. Banks said he was delighted to be asked to be president of the Supporters' Trust. 'What has impressed me is how many people have devoted their time and been actively involved in things like the work parties at the ground, or at the Cat & Fiddle, where people

Alan Banks.

Jimmy Giles.

have slept in tents overnight. They are the ones I take my hat off to.

'Last year it was an absolute pleasure to go to the ground because they were playing some terrific football. To start with it was a learning curve and all about consolidation but after Christmas everyone began to realise, "We might have a chance here". I don't know whether Paul Tisdale is a genius or a lucky b*****d. Some of his selections and substitutions made me think, "I can't quite believe this", but they came off.

'The club has been badly run in the past and there was never any money. The only person who kept the club going was Ivor Doble and he told me it had cost him £1 million over the years. The Manchester United game saved the club but Exeter are very lucky because they have 2,500-3,000 really loyal supporters who go week in, week out. The euphoria at being in Division One is fantastic, but it is their reward for that loyalty.'

Jimmy Giles is another City stalwart and a plain-speaking summariser for Radio Devon who found himself having to pass comment on a lot of unappetising football. 'I really wasn't enjoying the Conference because the opposition would just come and shut up shop. I have always loved going to the club because of the social side but for a time the football wasn't entertaining.'

Giles was a centre-half but loves to see width in the team. 'Dean Moxey was great at getting forward and getting crosses in. Paul Tisdale has never signed star players or spent great money but he has a knack of taking journeymen players, who have often had three or four clubs, and moulding them into a good outfit, but it's a real team effort.'

'There were some great occasions, like at Oxford in the play-offs and going to Wembley for the first time, but it was such a relief to get back into the Football League. I always thought that if we finished halfway up League Two we would have done well, but the fact that we got promotion playing a lot of good football is a credit to the management at the club. The support we get in this part of the country is fantastic and those supporters – and all the volunteers at the club – really deserve it.'

'This was the right club for me. In football there are a lot of good clubs and a lot of good managers, but it is getting the fit. I think I have fitted in with what the club wanted and the club has suited me.'

Paul Tisdale
July 2009

Exeter's League Record under Paul Tisdale

Nationwide Conference 2006/07

A	York City	0-0	
H	Forest Green Rovers	1-0	Stansfield
H	Altrincham	2-1	Todd, Challinor
A	Tamworth	0-1	
H	Crawley	1-1	Moxey
A	Cambridge U	3-1	Phillips, Challinor, Crichton (og)
H	Aldershot T	0-0	
A	Oxford U	0-1	
A	Gravesend U	2-2	Edwards, Smith (og)
H	St Albans	4-2	Cozic, Gill, Phillips, Jones B (pen)
H	Stevenage	1-1	Jones B
A	Southport	1-0	Buckle
A	Grays Athletic	2-2	Challinor, Jones B
H	Halifax	4-1	Challinor 2, Stansfield, Mackie
H	Northwich	1-1	Phillips
A	Morecambe	2-2	Mackie, Stansfield
H	Stafford R	1-2	Stansfield
A	Woking	2-0	Buckle, Mackie
H	Kidderminster	1-1	Jones B
A	Burton	0-1	
H	Dagenham	3-2	Stansfield, Mackie, Blackett (og)
A	Weymouth	1-2	Jones B
A	St Albans	2-1	Carlisle, Moxey

2007

H	Oxford U	2-1	Brevett (og), Mackie
H	Gravesend	1-3	Challinor
H	Weymouth	4-0	Elam 3, Challinor
A	Dagenham	1-4	Carlisle

Goalscoring left-back Billy Jones.

A	Stafford	1-0	Phillips
H	Woking	1-0	Challinor
A	Kidderminster	2-0	Challinor, Elam
H	Rushden & D	0-0	
H	Burton	3-0	Jones B (pen), Logan (pen), Stansfield
A	Rushden & D	0-3	
H	Grays Athletic	2-1	Buckle, Jones B
A	Halifax T	1-2	Jones B
H	Morecambe	1-0	Logan
A	Northwich V	0-1	
H	York City	1-1	Jones B (pen),
A	Forest Green Rovers	1-2	Elam
A	Altrincham	2-1	Logan, Jones B (pen)
A	Aldershot T	2-3	Elam, Seaborne
H	Tamworth	1-0	Carlisle
A	Crawley T	3-0	Elam, Carlisle 2
H	Cambridge U	2-0	Logan, Stansfield
A	Stevenage	0-0	
H	Southport	2-1	Stansfield 2

Play-offs

H	Oxford	0-1	
A	Oxford	2-1	(won on pens) Phillips, Stansfield

Wembley

	Morecambe	1-2	Phillips

		P	W	D	L	Pts
1	Dagenham & R	46	28	11	7	95
2	Oxford Utd	46	22	15	9	81
3	Morecambe	46	23	12	11	81
4	York City	46	23	11	12	80
5	**Exeter City**	**46**	**22**	**12**	**12**	**78**
6	Burton Albion	46	22	9	15	75
7	Gravesend & N	46	21	11	14	74
8	Stevenage B	46	20	10	16	70
9	Aldershot T	46	18	11	17	65
10	Kidderminster H	46	17	12	17	63
11	Weymouth	46	18	9	19	63
12	Rushden & D	46	17	11	18	62
13	Northwich V	46	18	4	24	58
14	Forest Green R	46	13	18	15	57
15	Woking	46	15	12	19	57
16	Halifax Town	46	15	10	21	55
17	Cambridge Utd	46	15	10	21	55
18	Crawley Town	46	17	12	17	53
19	Grays Athletic	46	13	13	20	52
20	Stafford R	46	14	10	22	52
21	Altrincham	46	13	12	21	51
22	Tamworth	46	13	9	24	48
23	Southport	46	11	14	21	47
24	St Albans City	46	10	10	26	40

Most appearances: Gill 49

Leading goalscorer: Jones B 10 (4 pens)

Points split: 23 games, 36 points; 46 games, 78 points

Blue Square Conference 2007/08

A	Altrincham	4-1	Taylor M, Logan, Basham, Elam
H	Crawley T	2-0	Stansfield, Thomas (og)
H	York C	1-1	Logan (pen)
A	Droylesden	3-2	Moxey 2, Elam
H	Weymouth	0-0	
A	Kidderminster	0-4	
A	Oxford U	2-2	Logan 2
H	Cambridge U	1-1	Mackie
A	Farsley C	2-0	Stansfield, Logan (pen)
H	Forest Green R	3-3	Logan 2, Mackie
H	Ebbsfleet	1-1	Mackie
A	Woking	1-1	Lorraine (og)
A	Aldershot	0-2	
H	Grays Ath	1-0	Logan
H	Salisbury	4-2	Logan 3, Taylor M
A	Northwich Vic	0-0	
H	Rushden & D	2-2	Hatswell (og), Mackie
A	Stafford R	5-1	Carlisle, Taylor M 2, Mackie, Basham (pen)
H	Burton A	1-4	Mackie
A	Histon	2-2	Moxey, Mackie
A	Halifax T	3-0	Logan (pen), Elam, Mackie
H	Torquay U	4-3	Mackie 2, Moxey, Carlisle
H	Histon	2-1	Mackie, Cambridge (og)

2008

A	Torquay	0-1	
H	Oxford U	2-0	Stansfield 2
A	Forest Green R	1-1	Carlisle
A	Cambridge U	1-0	Seaborne
H	Stevenage B	4-0	Taylor M, Basham, Stansfield 2
A	Ebbsfleet	1-1	Gill
H	Woking	2-2	Taylor M 2
A	Grays Ath	2-0	Carlisle, Stansfield
H	Farsley C	2-1	Seaborne, Taylor M
H	Altrincham	2-1	Stansfield, Gill
A	Crawley T	2-2	Edwards, Moxey
A	York C	2-3	Basham, Logan
H	Kidderminster T	1-0	Gill
A	Weymouth	1-3	Taylor M
H	Halifax T	1-0	Logan
H	Droylsden	1-1	Logan (pen)
A	Stevenage B	1-0	Basham

A	Salisbury C	0-2	
H	Northwich Vic	2-1	Logan 2
H	Aldershot T	1-1	Stansfield
A	Rushden & D	2-0	Stansfield, Harley
H	Stafford R	4-1	Moxey 3, Watson
A	Burton A	4-4	Moxey, Stansfield, Friend, Logan

Play-offs

H	Torquay U	1-2	Carlisle
A	Torquay	4-1	Harley, Watson (pen), Logan, Carlisle

Wembley

Cambridge	1-0	Edwards

Most appearances: Edwards 49

Leading goalscorer: Logan 19 (4 pens)

Points split: 23 games, 40 points; 46 games, 83 points

		P	W	D	L	Pts
1	Aldershot T	46	31	8	7	101
2	Cambridge Utd	46	25	11	10	86
3	Torquay Utd	46	26	8	12	86
4	**Exeter City**	**46**	**22**	**17**	**7**	**83**
5	Burton Albion	46	23	12	11	81
6	Stevenage B	46	24	7	15	79
7	Histon	46	20	12	14	72
8	Forest Green R	46	19	14	13	71
9	Oxford Utd	46	20	11	15	71
10	Grays Athletic	46	19	13	14	70
11	Ebbsfleet Utd	46	19	12	15	69
12	Salisbury City	46	18	14	14	68
13	Kidderminster H	46	19	10	17	67
14	York City	46	17	11	18	62
15	Crawley Town	46	19	9	18	60
16	Rushden & D	46	15	14	17	59
17	Woking	46	12	17	17	53
18	Weymouth	46	11	13	22	46
19	Northwich V	46	11	11	24	44
20	Halifax Town	46	12	16	18	42
21	Altrincham	46	9	14	23	41
22	Farsley Celtic	46	10	9	27	39
23	Stafford Rangers	46	5	10	31	25
24	Droylsden	46	5	9	32	24

Wayne Carlisle celebrates scoring against Torquay.

Coca-Cola Football League Division Two 2008/09

A	Darlington	1-1	Seaborne
H	Shrewsbury	0-1	
A	Bournemouth	1-0	Harley
H	Luton	0-1	
H	Accrington	2-1	Gill, Watson
A	Bradford	1-4	Gill
H	Notts Co	2-2	Gill, Taylor
A	Macclesfield T	4-1	Gill, Harley, Stansfield 2
H	Gillingham	3-0	Logan, Stansfield 2
A	Bury	1-0	Logan
H	Grimsby T	0-0	
A	Port Vale	3-1	Gill, Sercombe, Stewart
A	Barnet	1-0	Gill
H	Chesterfield	1-6	Stansfield
H	Chester	2-0	Stansfield, Taylor
A	Aldershot T	0-1	
A	Morecambe	1-1	Panther
H	Rotherham	1-1	Watson
H	Lincoln	2-1	McAllister, Moxey
H	Rochdale	4-1	Basham 2 (1 pen), McAllister 2
A	Wycombe	1-1	Panther
H	Brentford	0-2	

Goalkeepers' union: Andy Marriott, coach Mel Gwinnett and Paul Jones.

2009

A	Notts Co	1-2	Stewart (pen)
H	Bury	0-0	
A	Dagenam & R	2-1	McAllister 2
A	Gillingham	0-1	
A	Chesterfield	1-2	Moxey
H	Barnet	2-1	Saunders, Gill
A	Grimsby	2-2	Stewart, Harley
H	Macclesfield	4-0	Stansfield, Logan, Saunders, McAllister
H	Aldershot T	3-2	Stewart, Sandell (og), Saunders
A	Chester C	0-0	
H	Darlington	2-0	Gill (pen), McAllister
A	Shrewsbury T	1-1	Stewart
A	Luton T	2-1	Stansfield, Sercombe
H	Bournemouth	1-3	Stansfield
H	Bradford C	1-0	Moxey
A	Accrington S	1-2	Stansfield
A	Rochdale	2-2	Stewart 2 (1 pen)
H	Port Vale	1-0	Prosser (og)
H	Dagenham & R	2-1	Fleetwood 2
A	Brentford	1-1	Fleetwood
H	Wycombe	1-0	Gill
A	Lincoln	1-0	Burch (og)
H	Morecambe	2-2	Moxey, Harley
A	Rotherham	1-0	Logan

		P	W	D	L	Pts
1	Brentford	46	23	16	7	85
2	**Exeter City**	**46**	**22**	**13**	**11**	**79**
3	Wycombe W	46	20	18	8	78
4	Bury	46	21	15	10	78
5	Gillingham	46	21	12	13	75
6	Rochdale	46	19	13	14	70
7	Shrewsbury T	46	17	18	11	69
8	Dagenham & R	46	19	11	16	68
9	Bradford City	46	18	13	15	67
10	Chesterfield	46	16	15	15	63
11	Morecambe	46	15	18	13	63
12	Darlington	46	20	12	14	62
13	Lincoln City	46	14	17	15	59
14	Rotherham Utd	46	21	12	13	58
15	Aldershot Town	46	14	12	20	54
16	Accrington S	46	13	11	22	50
17	Barnet	46	11	15	20	48
18	Port Vale	46	13	9	24	48
19	Notts County	46	11	14	21	47
20	Macclesfield T	46	13	8	25	47
21	Bournemouth	46	17	12	17	46
22	Grimsby Town	46	9	14	23	41
23	Chester City	46	8	13	25	37
24	Luton Town	46	13	17	16	26

Most appearances: Jones 46

Leading goalscorer: Stansfield 10

Points split: 23 games, 36 points; 46 games, 79 points

Exeter City's league record, 2006–09

(combined)

P	W	D	L	F	A	Pts
138	66	42	30	215	156	240

Exeter City average home attendances

2002/03	3,511
2003/04	3,417
2004/05	3,494
2005/06	3,520
2006/07	3,753
2007/08	3,709
2008/09	4,940

Paul Tisdale's Transfer Trail

(1 July 2006 – 30 June 2009)

IN

Patrick Ada	(St Albans)
Bertie Cozic	(Team Bath)
Rob Edwards	(Blackpool)
Jon Richardson	(Forest Green Rovers)
Wayne Carlisle	(free agent)
Steve Tully	(Weymouth)
Lee Elam	(Weymouth)
Richard Logan	(Weymouth)
Matt Taylor	(Team Bath)
Steve Basham	(Oxford United)
Andy Marriott	(Boston United)
Neil Saunders	(Team Bath)
Frankie Artus	(Bristol City, loan)
Ryan Harley	(Weston-super-Mare)
Ben Watson	(Grays Athletic, initially on loan)
Craig McAllister	(Oxford United)
Marcus Stewart	(Yeovil Town)
Manny Panther	(York City)
Jack Obersteller	(Wycombe Wanderers)
Nick Jordan	(Portsmouth)
Ronnie Bull	(Fisher Athletic)
Fred Murray	(Stevenage)
Troy Archibald-Henville	(Tottenham Hotspur, loan)
Alex Russell	(Cheltenham, initially on loan)
Stuart Fleetwood	(Charlton Athletic, loan)

OUT

Danny Woodards	(Crewe Alexandra, £30,000)
Patrick Ada	(St Albans, loan)
Patrick Ada	(Histon)
Danny Clay	(Salisbury)
Released:	Chris Wright, Steven Hunt
Paul Buckle	(Torquay)
Lee Phillips	(Torquay, £17,500)
Chris Todd	(Torquay, £7,500)
Martin Rice	(Torquay)
Billy Jones	(Crewe Alexandra, £65,000)
Jamie Mackie	(Plymouth Argyle, £145,00)
Luke Cole	(Stevenage)
Jon Richardson	(retired)
Wayne Carlisle	(Torquay United)
Andy Taylor	(Weymouth)
Lee Elam	(Altrincham)
George Friend	(Wolverhampton Wanderers, £350,000)
Matt Gill	(Norwich City)
Dean Moxey	(Derby County, £350,000)
Released:	Steve Basham, Jack Obersteller, Ronnie Bull, Fred Murray, Nick Jordan, Toby Osman